THE MIDDLE WAY

THE MIDDLE WAY

FAITH GROUNDED IN REASON

THE DALAI LAMA

TRANSLATED BY THUPTEN JINPA

WISDOM PUBLICATIONS • BOSTON

Wisdom Publications
199 Elm Street
Somerville MA 02144 USA
www.wisdompubs.org
In association with the Canadian Tibetan Association of Ontario.

Library of Congress Cataloging-in-Publication Data
Bstan-'dzin-rgya-mtsho, Dalai Lama XIV, 1935–
  Middle way : faith grounded in reason / the Dalai Lama ; translated, Thupten Jinpa.
    p. cm.
  Includes bibliographical references and index.
  ISBN 0-86171-552-7 (hardcover : alk. paper)
  I. Madhyamika (Buddhism) I. Thupten Jinpa. II. Title.
  BQ7462.B79 2009
  294.3'42042--dc22
                                    2009008855

13 12 11 10 09
5 4 3 2 1

Cover design by Rick Snizik. Interior design by TLLC. Set in Centaur MT 12/17. Photos of the Dalai Lama © 2009 Don Farber.

Contents

Translator's Preface

This book, based on a series of important Buddhist teachings His Holiness the Dalai Lama conferred in Toronto in 2004, presents a comprehensive explanation of the foundational teachings of Mahayana Buddhism as they are understood in the Tibetan tradition. The teaching in this book is divided into two broad sections. The first section presents the Buddhist path to enlightenment based on an explanation of three key chapters from *Fundamental Stanzas on the Middle Way* (*Mulamadhyamakakarika*) by the second-century Indian teacher Nagarjuna; the second section presents the way to put the understanding of the key elements of the Buddhist path into practice. This second section is based on the *Three Principal Aspects of the Path*, a lucid verse work originally written as a letter of instruction by Jé Tsongkhapa (1357–1419) to a student in a distant land. These two important classical texts are separated by nearly a millennium and a half yet complement each other beautifully. That both speak so profoundly even to the spiritual aspirant at the beginning of this third millennium demonstrates the universality and timelessness of the insights they embody.

As on numerous occasions in the past, I had the honor of being the Dalai Lama's translator when these teachings were delivered. Right from the first day, I noticed something unique about this particular series of teachings. Unlike on many other occasions,

His Holiness was proceeding through the texts in a particularly systematic fashion. He did this, in part, to substantiate his oft-repeated statement that Tibetan Buddhism is a direct continuation of the scholastic lineage of Nalanda Monastery in the Indian Buddhist tradition. Before Buddhism disappeared from central India, Nalanda was the most important Buddhist monastery there, thriving from early in the Common Era to the end of the twelfth century. The Dalai Lama began his presentation in Toronto by citing a text he himself composed to honor the key Nalanda masters whose teachings lay at the heart of the Tibetan Buddhist tradition (the full text of which can be found in appendix 2 of this volume):

> Today, in an age when science and technology have reached a most advanced stage, we are incessantly preoccupied with mundane concerns. In such an age, it is crucial that we who follow the Buddha attain faith in his teaching on the basis of genuine understanding. It is with an objective mind endowed with a curious skepticism that we should engage in careful analysis and seek the reasons [behind our beliefs]. Then, on the basis of seeing the reasons, we engender a faith that is accompanied by wisdom.

A central aspect of what the Dalai Lama calls the Nalanda tradition is an emphasis on approaching the Buddhadharma not just through faith and devotion but also through critical inquiry. This approach, known as the "way of the intelligent person," is emphasized in the writings of numerous Nalanda masters. The faith in the Buddha and his teaching—the Dharma—that is engendered in such a manner is unshakable and is of the highest kind. So, how do we go about developing such an unshakable faith? The Dalai Lama writes:

> By understanding the two truths, the nature of the ground,
> I will ascertain how, through the four truths, we enter and
>   exit samsara;
> I will make firm the faith in the Three Jewels that is born of
>   knowledge.
> May I be blessed so that the root of the liberating path is
>   firmly established within me.

This stanza from His Holiness's *Praise to Seventeen Nalanda Masters* provides, in a sense, the structure of the first part of this book, the explanation of key elements of the Buddhist path through a commentary on Nagarjuna's *Fundamental Stanzas on the Middle Way*. The Dalai Lama first gives a commentary on Nagarjuna's chapter on the twelve links of dependent origination, which is the twenty-sixth chapter of that text. That chapter presents in detail the Buddhist understanding of the causal processes that lock us in the cycle of existence. At the root of this cycle of twelve links is fundamental ignorance, which grasps at the inherent realness of our own selves and the world around us.

This is followed by a commentary on chapter 18, which presents Nagarjuna's understanding of the Buddha's teaching on "no-self" (*anatman*), the selflessness of both the person as well as the five psychophysical components of the person. It is this chapter that presents the teaching on emptiness, which, according to Nagarjuna, is the ultimate mode of being of all things. This emptiness, to use

Nagarjuna's own words, is *tathata* ("thatness"), *paramartha* ("the ultimate truth"), and *dharmata* ("reality itself").

Finally, in his commentary on Nagarjuna's chapter 24, the Dalai Lama explains how Nagarjuna's teaching on emptiness is not a form of nihilism but is, in fact, the understanding of reality that enables us to account for conventional reality. Only this explanation of emptiness makes the operations of cause and effect tenable. His Holiness explains how in Nagarjuna's system, emptiness—the ultimate truth—and dependent origination—the relative truth—are inseparably intertwined.

By weaving together lucid exposition and penetrating analysis, along with the insights of such authoritative commentators as Aryadeva (ca. second century), Chandrakirti (seventh century), and Tsongkhapa (writing in the early fifteenth century), the Dalai Lama allows the verses of Nagarjuna's text to reveal their deep insight into the nature of existence. Throughout, the Dalai Lama never loses the sight that, in the final analysis, the teachings on emptiness are meant to be related to our personal experience and bring a deeper understanding of the world around us. As Nagarjuna puts it, the purpose of the emptiness teaching is to pacify grasping at an inherent existence of both our own self and all phenomena so that we may gain genuine freedom.

The second part of this book presents the methods to put the understanding of the Buddhist path into practice. Here, His Holiness offers a beautiful explanation of Tsongkhapa's well-known *Three Principal Aspects of the Path*, the three aspects being true renunciation, the altruistic awakening mind, and the correct view of emptiness. Having cultivated a reliable understanding of the Buddhist path based on critical reflection on the teachings on emptiness, the four noble truths, and the twelve links of dependent origination, one could then use this second section of the book as a manual for daily meditation.

In editing the transcript for this book, I have greatly enjoyed encountering this unique series of teachings anew. Numerous people have helped make this work possible. First of all, I am profoundly grateful to His Holiness himself for always being such a wellspring of Buddhist wisdom and compassion. I thank the Tibetan Canadian Association of Ontario, especially its president, Norbu Tsering, for organizing the 2004 Kalachakra initiation in Toronto that provided the occasion for His Holiness's teachings presented in this book; Lyna de Julio and Linda Merle for their help in transcribing parts of the teachings; and Ven. Lhakdor and his team in Dharamsala at the Central Archives of His Holiness the Dalai Lama for providing me a Tibetan transcript of His Holiness's teaching, which proved enormously helpful in revising and editing the transcript of my own oral English translation. Finally, I thank my editor at Wisdom Publications, David Kittelstrom, for his invaluable help in making the language of this book lucid and readable. May our efforts contribute to making the wisdom of the great Buddhist master Nagarjuna, through the inspiring words of His Holiness the Dalai Lama, a source of insight and inspiration to many seekers on the path to awakening.

Thupten Jinpa
Montreal, 2009

Prologue

THE POWER OF COMPASSION

Many centuries ago, humans realized the importance of harnessing the intellect. From that evolved writing and, eventually, formal education. These days, it is a truism to say that education is vital, but it is important to remind ourselves of the larger purpose of education. After all, what good is the accumulation of knowledge if it does not lead to a happier life?

We've all come across people who have received an excellent education but who are not very happy. Education may have brought them more critical thinking power and greater expectations, but they have had difficulty actualizing all those expectations, leading to anxiety and frustration. Clearly, education alone does not guarantee a happier life. I think of education like an instrument, one that we can use for either constructive or destructive ends.

You might think that the goal of education is merely to augment one's ability to increase one's wealth, possessions, or power. But just as mere knowledge in and of itself is not sufficient to make us happy, material things or power alone also cannot overcome worry and frustration. There must be some other factor in our minds that creates the foundation for a happy life, something that allows us to handle life's difficulties effectively.

I

I usually describe myself as a simple Buddhist monk, and my own formal education has not been that extensive. I know something about Buddhist philosophy and texts, but I was a rather lazy student during my early years of study, so my knowledge of even that field is limited. On top of that, I learned next to nothing of fields like mathematics or world history or geography. In addition, as a young person, I led a fairly comfortable life. The Dalai Lamas were not millionaires, but still my life was comfortable. So when the Chinese invaded and I had to flee my native land, I had only some limited knowledge of Buddhist teachings, and I had little experience of dealing with problems. A great burden and responsibility was thrust upon me suddenly, and what training I had was put to the test. During those years, my most reliable friend was my own inner quality of compassion.

Compassion brings inner strength, and compassion also brings truth. With truth, you have nothing to hide, and you are not dependent on the opinions of others. That brings a self-confidence, with which you can deal with any problem without losing hope or determination. Based on my experiences, I can say that when life becomes difficult and you are confronting a host of problems, if you maintain your determination and keep making an effort, then obstacles or problems become really very helpful, for they broaden and deepen your experience. Thus I think compassion is the most precious thing.

What is compassion? Compassion involves a feeling of closeness to others, a respect and affection that is not based on others' attitude toward us. We tend to feel affection for people who are important to us. That kind of close feeling does not extend to our enemies—those who think ill of us. Genuine compassion, on the other hand, sees that others, just like us, want a happy and successful life and do not want to suffer. That kind of feeling and concern can be extended to friend and enemy alike, regardless of their feelings toward us. That's genuine compassion.

Ordinary love is biased and mixed with attachment. Like other afflicted emotions, attachment is based not on reality but on mental projection. It exaggerates reality. In reality there may be some good there, but attachment views it as one hundred percent beautiful or good. Compassion gets much closer to reality. There is a vast difference.

The big question is whether we can cultivate such compassion. Based on my own experience, the answer is yes. It is possible because we all possess the seed of compassion as the very nature of our human existence. Likewise, our very survival as human beings, especially in our first few years of life, is heavily dependent on the affection and compassion of others. We have survived up to now only because at the beginning of our lives, our mother—or someone else, of course—cared. Had she been negligent even one or two days, we would have died. As human beings, using our intelligence, we can extend this sense of caring throughout our whole lives.

The need to systematically cultivate and enhance this natural capacity is today more urgent than ever. In modern times, due to population, technology, and the modern economy, the world is now deeply interconnected. The world is becoming much smaller. Despite political, ideological, and in some cases religious differences, people around the world have to work and live together. That's reality. So the role of compassion on the international level is vital.

Every day, the media brings news of bloodshed and terrorist activities. These events do not come to pass without causes or conditions.

Some of the events we face today I think have roots in negligent actions in the eighteenth, nineteenth, and twentieth centuries. And unfortunately, there are some who deliberately try to escalate people's vengeful urges for political gain. What is the best way to face this violence? I would argue that it is not through more violence and bloodshed. Problems rooted in violence cannot be solved by violence.

Why is this? Firstly, violence by its nature is unpredictable. You may start out with a certain goal of "limited" violence, but then it gets out of control. Secondly, violence harms others, and violence therefore creates more hatred in others' minds. That in turn creates the seeds for future problems. War is like a legalized outlet for violence. In ancient times, when countries were less dependent on each other, the destruction of an enemy could be construed as victory for oneself. But today, due to the profound interconnectedness of all nations, war is ineffective. The destruction of your enemy just ends up destroying yourself.

Therefore, when we encounter conflict or competing interests, the best way—indeed the only effective way—to solve it is through dialogue. You must respect others' interests, others' desires, and make compromises, because if you neglect others' interests, ultimately you yourself will suffer. You must take care of others' interests.

I often tell audiences that the twentieth century was a century of violence, and through that experience we now know that violence cannot solve problems. The only way to solve them is with peaceful resolution. Therefore, the twenty-first century should be the century of dialogue. For that, we need determination, patience, and a broader perspective. Again, this is where compassion has an important role. First, as I mentioned, it brings us self-confidence. Compassion brings us deep recognition of others' rights. Compassion also gives us a calm mind, and with a calm mind, we can see reality more clearly. When our mind is dominated by afflictive emotions, we can't see reality, and we make poor decisions. Compassion gives us a more holistic view.

I respect the world's political leaders, but sometimes I think they should have more compassion. If even one of these political leaders cultivates more compassion, then millions of innocent people get more peace. Many years ago, at an official function in India, I met a politician from the Indian state of East Bengal. The meeting included a discussion of ethics and spirituality, and he said, "As a politician I don't know much about those things." He was probably just being humble, but I gently chided him. Politicians need more ethics, more spirituality, I said. If a religious practitioner in a remote area does something harmful, it probably doesn't have much global effect. But when leaders and politicians are not mindful and compassionate, it is very dangerous.

I believe compassion is not a religious matter. Some people think compassion and forgiveness are the domains of religion, and if people have a negative view of religion they may become negative about these things as well. That's a mistake. Whether we accept a religion or not is up to the individual, but as long as humanity inhabits this world, these deeper values are crucial and must not be neglected. Everybody is making every effort for material prosperity. That's fine, but if in the meantime we neglect our inner world or inner values, we will not be happy. We must combine material development with the development of internal, human values. We need to develop respect, love, and a sense of compassion in order to have happier lives, happier families, happier communities, and finally a happier world. We need these inner qualities. This should be the ultimate goal of education today.

About this book

I do not believe that religion is necessary to develop ethics and a good heart. Nonetheless, the major world religions have over time developed many valuable tools for cultivating such universal human virtues. Buddhism is not alone in this respect, but it is the tradition with which I am most familiar, and I also believe that the Buddhist tradition contains unique elements, particularly its teachings on self-lessness, or emptiness, and on the nature of the mind. And so, part of my purpose in this book is to give you a good understanding of the overall framework of Buddhism.

I will first present a general introduction to the Buddhadharma, and to do this I've selected three chapters from Nagarjuna's *Fundamental Stanzas on the Middle Way*, a classical Indian philosophical work that contains twenty-seven chapters in all. As I explain the basic framework of the Buddhist path, I will relate my explanations to specific sections of these three chapters. The general introduction is then followed by an explanation on how to put these teachings into practice on the basis of Jé Tsongkhapa's short verse work, *Three Principal Aspects of the Path*. Tsongkhapa is the founder of the Geluk tradition of Tibetan Buddhism.

When teaching or listening to Buddhadharma, those who consider themselves practicing Buddhists need to do so with a pure motivation. The teacher must ensure that he or she does not conduct the teaching out of a desire for respect, fame, or financial reward; he or she must be motivated purely by the wish for the well-being of all sentient beings. As listeners, too, your motivation must not be polluted by aspirations for greatness as a scholar, high reputation, or financial reward; rather, you must listen to the teachings with the wish to turn your mind toward the Dharma, to make your Dharma practice successful, and to make your practice a cause for attaining liberation and the omniscient state of buddhahood.

How do we ensure the purity of our motivation when giving a teaching or listening to one? One way is by reciting special prayers of aspiration before we begin. Now, for a teaching to truly become Buddhist, it must be predicated on the practice of going for refuge in the Three Jewels—the Buddha, the Dharma, and the community of true practitioners. For a teaching to become a teaching of the Mahayana tradition—the bodhisattva path—it must be based on the generation of *bodhichitta,* the altruistic awakening mind, which strives for enlightenment for the purpose of benefiting others. To begin, then, we remind ourselves of these two practices of going for refuge and generating the altruistic awakening mind by chanting or reflecting on the following stanza:

> To the Buddha, Dharma, and the excellent assembly,
> I go for refuge until I am enlightened.
> Through pursuing the practices of giving and the other
>   perfections,
> may I attain buddhahood for the benefit of all beings.

When I give introductions to the Buddhadharma, non-Buddhists are always welcome to follow along in order to seek something beneficial. If among my explanations, you find that some are useful, incorporate them into your everyday life; those that are not so useful you can simply discard. However, in my explanations on Buddhist philosophy, many points of difference will naturally emerge, since I am presenting a Buddhist text that espouses, naturally, the Buddhist outlook. When this occurs, please don't feel that I am somehow disparaging your tradition.

Of course, historically, the great Buddhist scholars of India's Nalanda monastic university had extensive debates among themselves. Proponents of the Mind Only (*Chittamatra*) school, for example, criticized the Middle Way (*Madhyamaka*) position as falling into the extreme of nihilism, while proponents of the Middle Way school criticized the Mind Only position as falling into the extreme of absolutism. Therefore, in this regard, I share the sentiment of the eighteenth-century Tibetan master Changkya Rinpoché (1717–86) who wrote:

> It's not that I do not respect you;
> Please forgive me if I've offended.[1]

The Buddhism that flourished in Tibet is a comprehensive tradition. It contains all the essential elements of all the teachings of the Mahayana and Lesser Vehicle traditions, and on top of that includes the tantric teachings of the Vajrayana as well. From the standpoint of source languages, the Tibetan tradition encompasses many of the key texts in the Pali-language tradition, but is based primarily on the Sanskrit Indian tradition. In terms of the origin of its lineages, the tradition is most indebted to the great masters of Nalanda, the monastic institution that flourished in northern India during the first millennium. For example, the key texts studied in the Tibetan monastic colleges are all composed by the great Nalanda thinkers and adepts. I have actually composed a prayer, *Praise to Seventeen Nalanda Masters*, to acknowledge the origin of our tradition and the debt that we Tibetan Buddhists owe to their writings. The full text of this prayer appears at the end of this book. In the colophon to that, I wrote:

> Today, in an age when science and technology have reached a most advanced stage, we are incessantly preoccupied with mundane concerns. In such an age, it is crucial that we who follow the Buddha acquire faith in his teaching on the basis of genuine understanding.

It is out of this conviction that the ancient teachings of Buddhism are as relevant and valuable as ever that I present this introduction to the Tibetan tradition.

Part I

An Exploration of Nagarjuna's
Fundamental Stanzas
on the Middle Way

1. Approaching the Profound

Today, here in the twenty-first century, humanity has reached a highly advanced stage of material development and of knowledge of various fields, and we continue to progress in these areas. However, the demands on our attention are never-ending, and in such an environment, it is vital for the Buddhists to obtain genuine confidence in the Buddhadharma grounded in understanding and reason.

How do we go about obtaining a faith grounded in understanding? As I wrote in the colophon to *Praise to Seventeen Nalanda Masters,*

> It is with an objective mind endowed with a curious skepticism that we should engage in careful analysis and seek the reasons. Then, on the basis of seeing the reasons, we engender a faith that is accompanied by wisdom.

Now, whenever we engage in an analysis, such as on the nature of mind or reality, if we proceed from the start already convinced that "It *must* be so and so," then due to our biases, we will be unable to see the actual truth and will instead see only our naïve projection. It is therefore essential that the analyzing mind strive to be objective and not swayed by prejudices. What we need is a skeptical curiosity, our mind moving between the possibilities, genuinely wondering whether it is thus or some other way. We need to begin our analysis as objectively as possible.

However, if we maintain an objective stance unswayed by bias yet have no feeling or interest in the analysis, this too is incorrect. We should cultivate a *curious* mind, drawn toward all possibilities; and when we do, the desire to deeply investigate naturally arises. If this mind drawn toward possibilities is absent, we just abandon the inquiry and simply say, dismissively, "I don't know." This way, then, brings no real benefit because we are not open to new insights.

Therefore, a curious skepticism is extremely important. For where there is such skepticism, constant inquiry also takes place. One of the reasons science progresses is because it persistently inquires and performs experiments on the basis of a genuine objectivity, "Why is it like this?" with a curious mind that is drawn to all sorts of possibilities. In this way, the truth becomes clearer and clearer, allowing these truths to become correctly understood.

"Careful analysis" indicates that a rough or incomplete analysis is not adequate. For example, in the method of analysis presented in Buddhist logic and epistemology texts, it is not adequate to rely on a proof that is based only on partial observation of a fact, on additional observation of the fact in a similar class, or on mere nonobservation of the fact in any dissimilar class. To base your conclusion on such partial grounds is inadequate. Buddhist logic and epistemology texts emphasize the need for proving the truth of an assertion based on sound reasoning rooted in direct observation. With a careful analysis, our conclusions are more stable and sound.

As we become more aware and understand the reasoning presented in a text, these should be related back to our own personal experiences. Ultimately, the final proof is a direct valid experience.

Buddhist texts speak of four types or qualities of intelligence: great intelligence, swift intelligence, clear intelligence, and penetrating intelligence. Because we must analyze the subject matter carefully, we need *great intelligence;* because we cannot naïvely conclude that something is the case except on the basis of a meticulous analysis, we needs *clear intelligence;* because we need to be able to "think on our feet," we need *swift intelligence;* and because we need to pursue the full implications of a line of inquiry, we need *penetrating intelligence.*

By analyzing in such a manner and seeking what consequences and significance we can draw from our understanding, we will come to see those results. Here, we must first systematically organize the lines of reasoning presented in the texts and then correlate these with our own personal experience so that the reasoning is supported by direct observation and empirical evidence. When, on the basis of relating these lines of reasoning to our own personal experience, we feel "Yes, they are truly helpful" or "This is truly wonderful," we have gained a decisive sense of conviction in the Buddhadharma. Such a confidence is called a faith grounded in genuine understanding.

SEQUENCE OF ANALYSIS

As for the actual sequence of engaging in analysis, in *Praise to Seventeen Nalanda Masters,* I wrote:

> By understanding the two truths, the nature of the ground,
> I will ascertain how, through the four truths, we enter and
>   exit samsara;
> I will make firm the faith in the Three Jewels that is born of
>   knowledge.

> May I be blessed so that the root of the liberating path is
> firmly established within me.

Here, when we speak of practicing the Buddhadharma, we are
speaking of observing the ethics of refraining from ten nonvirtues
and cultivating compassion and loving-kindness within a context of
seeking liberation. Merely refraining from the ten nonvirtues or cultivating of compassion and loving-kindness alone do not constitute
a specific practice of the Buddhadharma; such practices of ethics
and compassion are, after all, a feature of many spiritual traditions.
When we speak of Buddhadharma in this context, the term *Dharma*
(or spirituality) refers to the peace of *nirvana*—liberation—and to
definite goodness, a term that encompasses both liberation from samsara
as well as the full enlightenment of buddhahood. We use the term
definite goodness because the peace of nirvana is utterly excellent, pure,
and everlasting. When practices such as avoiding unwholesome,
harming actions and cultivating love and compassion are part of a
quest for gaining liberation from cyclic existence, then they truly
become Dharma in the sense of being Buddhist spiritual activity.

"Liberation" here is defined as the cessation of the mind's pollutants through the power of applying their corresponding antidotes. The main pollutant, the very root of our unenlightened
existence, is the grasping at selfhood, at self-existence, and all the
associated psychological and emotional factors that accompany and
proceed from grasping at self-existence. The direct antidote to the
self-grasping mind as well its associated mental factors is insight
into selflessness. Therefore, it is on the basis of realizing selflessness
that we attain true liberation.

This is how the method of attaining definite goodness is presented, and the spiritual methods associated with the attainment of such liberation are the unique way of Buddhism. Therefore, I wrote, "May I be blessed so that the root of the liberating path is firmly established in me."

THE FOUR NOBLE TRUTHS

Now to establish the root of the path to liberation firmly within ourselves, it is essential to understand the four noble truths.[2] The four truths are like the foundation for all the Buddha's teachings—both sutra and tantra. When the Buddha first taught the Dharma to his earliest disciples, he taught the four noble truths.

If we reflect deeply upon the way in which the Buddha taught the four noble truths, we see that he first described their characteristics or nature, second their functions, and third the outcome that we will experience once they are realized directly. This is why, in Buddhist teachings, we often find discussions of the three main elements of ground, path, and result. The understanding of the nature of reality is the *ground,* the *path* is pursued based on the understanding of the ground, and finally the *result* is experienced as an effect of cultivating the path.

The Buddha's teaching on the four noble truths is a description of the actual nature of reality. When the Buddha taught the four truths, he began by describing their natures, saying, "This is the noble truth of suffering, this is the noble truth of the origin of suffering, this is the noble truth of the cessation of suffering, and this is the noble truth of the path." By declaring the truths in this way, the Buddha was making a statement about the way things exist; he was describing the nature of the ground.

Now, the "suffering" in the Buddha's first noble truth, in which he says, "This is the noble truth of suffering," includes all the sufferings that plague us. Within this there are many different levels of subtlety, not just the manifest suffering of pain and hardship but also a deeper and more pervasive quality of our experiences. The statement "This is the noble truth of suffering" recognizes that all these experiences are unsatisfactory, or "in the nature of suffering."

In the second truth, the statement "This is the noble truth of the origin of suffering" declares the cause that brings about suffering or that constitutes the source of suffering. Even though the origin of suffering is itself also a form of suffering and thus included in the first truth, suffering and its origin are here distinguished and described in the manner of a cause and an effect. Again, the primary cause of suffering that the Buddha identifies is our grasping at self-existence, the fundamental ignorance that distorts our view of reality and causes us to relate only to our confused appearances and not to the way things truly are.

The statement in the third noble truth, "This is the noble truth of cessation," declares the nature of freedom from suffering, its complete cessation. It states that the causes of suffering can be deliberately brought to an end. When the seeds of these causes become fewer and fewer and are finally eradicated, naturally the fruits that would otherwise have been produced and experienced cannot arise. So the statement here declares the possibility of a time when our suffering and its origin are totally pacified.

To fully understand the possibility of such a cessation, you cannot rely on your understanding of phenomena on the level of mere appearances; rather, you must penetrate their true mode of being. You cannot rely on the ordinary level of appearances because they are unreliable. The very root cause of your suffering, fundamental ignorance, is deluded about the true mode of being of phenomena —the way things actually exist—and fundamental ignorance dominates every moment our present experience.

This fundamental ignorance, however, is not inextricably fused with the luminous nature of our minds. Ultimately, ignorance and the mind can be separated; ignorance is not inherent to the nature of our minds. Therefore, the statement in the fourth truth that "This is the noble truth of the path" declares that cessation can be realized within our mental continuum through certain methods. Foremost among these is the wisdom that realizes the nature of reality. To eliminate fundamental ignorance, we cultivate the knowledge of selflessness and meditate upon this truth. The path that directly realizes selflessness can directly attack the deluded mind that falsely perceives selfhood and eliminate it. In this way, the nature of the path is declared.

In brief, by enumerating the identity of the four truths, the Buddha taught the nature of the ground, the way things actually are, which is illustrated by the following analogy. When someone is ill with a curable condition, you have the suffering of the illness itself, the external and internal factors that gave rise to the illness, the potential for healing, and the remedy or medication that counters the illness's causes and brings about its cure. In the same manner, there is a path that leads to the cessation of all sufferings. This is the nature of the ground, the understanding of the way things actually are.

No one has to compel us to seek happiness and try to overcome suffering, and we don't need to logically prove the value of these two pursuits. The inclination to seek happiness and shun suffering

exists naturally in us all, even in animals. Just as this natural inclination to seek out happiness and avert suffering is a basic fact of our
reality, the four causally connected truths—suffering and its origin,
cessation and the path—are also basic facts of reality.

Now the question is, "Taking these facts as the basis, how do we
apply our knowledge of the four noble truths—our understanding
of the ground?" In response to this question, the Buddha answered,
"Recognize suffering, eliminate the origin of suffering, actualize
cessation, and cultivate the path." In this, his second enumeration of
the four noble truths, the Buddha taught their functions, the process
we must follow to actualize them in our own minds. Among the
threefold explanation (of ground, path, and result) this is the explanation of the path.

Now, when we come to recognize the sufferings thoroughly,
the wish to be free from such sufferings arises naturally. Therefore,
with the statement, "Recognize suffering," the Buddha taught the
importance of well understanding all the gross and subtle levels of
suffering. The contemplation of suffering proceeds by way of
three progressively more subtle varieties of suffering—evident suffering, changeable suffering, and the suffering of conditioning
itself. *Evident suffering*, which is also called the "suffering of suffering," is manifest pain and hardship—the worldly definition of suffering. *Changeable suffering* is conventionally understood as pleasure,
but its inherent instability, its impermanence, always brings suffering in its eventual wake. The subtlest level, the *suffering of conditioning*, is the very quality of all experience conditioned by
ignorance—painful, pleasurable, or otherwise. Whenever ignorance is a factor in our perception of reality—and for most people, that is all the time—then whatever actions we perform and

whatever experiences we have will be colored by the unease engendered by misperception.

In general, evident suffering is something even animals can recognize. We don't require extraordinary contemplation to develop the wish to be free from it. However, evident suffering comes on the basis of changeable suffering, which in turn is rooted in the suffering of conditioning. So though we may try and eliminate evident suffering alone, as long as the suffering of conditioning persists, evident suffering may come to be reduced but it cannot be eliminated. Therefore, to eliminate evident suffering entirely, we must eliminate the suffering of conditioning. Thus the meaning of the statement "Recognize suffering" is to recognize the suffering of conditioning.

Similarly, the meaning of the statement "Eliminate the origin of suffering" is to eliminate the root cause of all sufferings, which is fundamental ignorance. The meaning of the statement "Actualize cessation" is to cease suffering and its origin. This is what we must seek, the final objective we must aspire to—the *definite goodness* mentioned above.

Finally, "Cultivate the path" means that what is called *cessation* must be actualized within our own minds, and we must therefore train in the causes that will lead to its attainment. We must put our understanding into actual practice. In speaking of enlightened and unenlightened existence—samsara and nirvana—we are really talking about two different *states of mind.* As long as the mind remains in an unenlightened, deluded state, obscured by ignorance, we are in samsara or unenlightened existence. Once we gain insight into the true nature of reality and see through the deception of ignorance, the process of enlightenment begins. Hence samsara and nirvana, benightedness and enlightenment, are actually functions of whether we are ignorant of or have insight into the ultimate nature of reality. The heart of our journey to enlightenment is developing this insight.

In brief, having first declared the four noble truths, the Buddha then taught how to apply them, explaining the sequence we need to tread the path. The first step the Buddha advises us to take is to "Recognize suffering." The Buddha elaborates, saying, "Recognize suffering, but there is no suffering to be recognized; eliminate the origin of suffering, but there is no origin of suffering to be eliminated; actualize cessation, but there is no cessation to be actualized; cultivate the path, but there is no path to be cultivated." With these statements, the Buddha evoked how knowledge of the four noble truths can reach its culmination—the result of the path. At the path's fruition, we no longer need to recognize any further suffering or to eliminate any further origin of suffering. This reality is the final realization of the four noble truths.

This is how the Buddha presented the four truths in terms of the ground, the path, and the result.

When the Buddha taught the four noble truths, he spoke of two sets of cause and effect—suffering and its origin on the one hand, and cessation and its cause, namely the path, on the other. The first cause and effect pertains to afflicted phenomena—to our rebirth within cyclic existence—while the second cause and effect pertains to enlightened phenomena—to the state where suffering is totally eliminated. The causes and effects of the afflicted class have ignorance as their root, whereas enlightened cause and effect proceeds through the cessation of fundamental ignorance—the purging of afflicted cause and effect. We see here again that both cyclic existence and its transcendence—samsara and nirvana—are defined in terms of knowledge or ignorance of the ultimate nature of reality. And again we see that the difference between samsara and nirvana is a difference in how we perceive reality.

A HIERARCHY OF VIEWS

The four noble truths are accepted by all schools of Buddhism. But to fully understand the subtle aspects of this central teaching, you need to grasp the teaching from the perspective of the most advanced presentation—because without a correct understanding of the nature of reality, you will not achieve a complete cessation of suffering. The highest and most subtle teaching on the correct view is found in the Middle Way school.

Since spiritual trainees have such different levels of intelligence, the Buddha, when explaining the ultimate nature of reality, first spoke of the gross level of ignorance. Later, to benefit spiritual trainees of medium and advanced mental aptitude, he spoke of the subtle level of ignorance. In the Buddhist scriptures, therefore, you can find explanations of ignorance or of ultimate reality at various levels of subtlety, depending on the audience the Buddha was addressing. From a philosophical standpoint, the subtle explanations he gave are more definitive than the grosser explanations.

If you engage in an analysis, using the reasoning process taught in the Middle Way treatises, then the presentations of the ultimate nature of reality found in the lower philosophical schools are revealed to be contradictory and undermined by reason. Of course the other schools leveled critiques of the Middle Way standpoint as well, but these critiques fail to fully comprehend the true nature of things. Nothing in their objections is grounded in a comprehensive understanding that can demonstrate any logical contradiction in the Middle Way standpoint. Therefore, while both are equal in having been taught by the blessed Buddha, those sacred words whose meaning is free from any defects when subjected to critical analysis must be accepted as definitive.

The Buddha himself stressed the need to analyze his words with an objective mind of curious skepticism. The Buddha stated:

> O monks and wise ones,
> like gold that is heated, cut, and rubbed,
> examine well my words
> and accept them, but not out of your reverence.[3]

It is because the Buddha took into account the diversity of the mental faculties, inclinations, and interests of his disciples that he gave such diverse teachings. Thus within Buddhist teachings, it is important to distinguish between teachings that are provisional and present provisional truths and those that are definitive and can be accepted at face value. It is the view of the Middle Way school that can be upheld with a deep sense of satisfaction, for the ultimate nature of reality identified in this view is not vulnerable to refutation, no matter how much it is subjected to critical analysis. Scriptures that present the Middle Way view, therefore, are considered definitive.

To speak of the four noble truths according to the Middle Way understanding, then, is to speak of two levels of the four noble truths—a gross level and a subtle level. Since the Buddha made both gross and subtle presentations of fundamental ignorance and the nature of reality, the four noble truths likewise have a gross presentation, which is based on the provisional teachings that the Buddha gave, and a subtle presentation, which draws on his definitive teachings on the nature of reality.

THE TWO TRUTHS

The great master Nagarjuna states in his *Fundamental Stanzas on the Middle Way* that:

> Teachings given by the Buddha
> are purely based on two truths.[4]

To understand the presentation of the four noble truths in accord with the Middle Way view, it is essential to understand these two levels of truth—conventional and ultimate. For as we have seen, without understanding the ultimate truth—the true mode of being of things—it is extremely difficult to posit cessation in all its comprehensiveness. This is why I wrote,

> By understanding the two truths, the nature of the ground,
> I will ascertain how, through the four truths, we enter and
>   exit samsara.

And since it is on the basis of understanding the two truths that we understand fully the nature of the Dharma Jewel, and on this basis, gain deeper understanding of the natures of the Buddha Jewel and the Sangha Jewel, I wrote:

I will make firm the faith in the Three Jewels that is born of
   knowledge;
may I be blessed so that the root of the liberating path is
   firmly established within me.

In other words, may a firm confidence in the Three Jewels arise in
me brought forth by true knowledge based on clear recognition of
the natures of the three objects of refuge; and on this basis may the
root of the path to liberation be firmly established in me.

The sequence I have delineated here is based on Maitreya's
approach in his *Ornament of Clear Realizations* (*Abhisamayalamkara*),
where, after generating the awakening mind, he presents the following instructions:

The practices and the [four noble] truths,
   as well as the Three Jewels such as the Buddha...⁵

In these lines Maitreya, in discussing the content of the practices, presents the instructions on the two truths, the instructions on the four noble truths—the framework of the
practices—and the instructions on the Three Jewels, which are
the support of the practices. I followed this same sequence in my
verse above.

   Now, the goals in Buddhism are the immediate aim of attaining
higher rebirth as a human being or as a god and the ultimate aim of
achieving definite goodness. The teachings on the means of attaining higher rebirth are based on cultivating "the right worldly view."
What is the right worldly view? It is the right view of the law of
karma and its effects based on conviction in the principle of

dependent origination. The goal sought and attained on the basis of such a view is higher rebirth.

If, on the other hand, we develop the understanding of the subtle meaning of how things exist as conceptual designations, we will then understand dependent origination to be empty, and on that basis, "the right *trans*worldly view" (as opposed to "the right *worldly* view) arises. The goal achieved as a result of this view is definite goodness. Therefore, even the goals of Buddhist spirituality are framed within the context of the two truths.

Furthermore, the highest definite goodness, the omniscient state of a buddha, is composed of two embodiments—the sublime body of form (*rupakaya*) and the sublime body of truth (*dharmakaya*). A buddha's form body is achieved through the accumulation of merit—the positive potential produced by pure acts of kindness, generosity, and other virtuous practices—while a buddha's truth body is achieved through the accumulation of wisdom, or insight into reality. Since we accumulate merit on the basis of the apparent aspect of dependent origination and accumulate wisdom on the basis of the empty aspect of dependent origination, it emerges that even the state of buddhahood is defined on the basis of the two truths. It is for these reasons it is stated that all the teachings the Buddha presented, however vast they may be, were taught within the framework of the two truths.

What are referred to as two truths are the two levels of reality, that of appearance and that of actual reality. Corresponding to these two levels is the understanding of the world that is grounded within the appearance level and the understanding of the world grounded within the level of actual reality, the way things truly are. In our day-to-day way of speaking, we recognize different levels of reality;

we make distinctions between appearances and reality, and we sense different levels of truth. The teachings of the two truths explicitly conceptualize our intuition of this difference. In this distinction that we experience between appearance and actual reality, the final, actual nature of things constitutes *ultimate truth*, while understanding developed within the framework of appearance, or of our everyday perception, constitutes *conventional truth*.

What then are the characteristics of the two truths? Conventional truths are facts of the world obtained by an understanding that is uncritical in regard to ultimate reality. Whenever we, not satisfied by the mere appearances discerned by an uncritical perspective, probe more deeply with critical analysis, searching for the true mode of being of things, the fact obtained through such an inquiry constitutes ultimate truth. This ultimate truth, the final nature of things, therefore, does not refer to some independent, self-standing absolute—some lofty ideal entity. Rather it refers to the final nature of a particular thing or phenomenon. The particular thing—the basis—and its true mode of being—its ultimate nature—constitute one and the same entity. Thus, although the perspectives or the characteristics of the two truths are defined distinctly, they pertain to one and the same reality. All phenomena, whatever they may be, possess each of these two truths.

2. *Twelve Links of Dependent Origination*

All schools of Buddhism speak of the principle of dependent origination (*pratitya samutpada*), namely that phenomena come into being in dependence upon other phenomena. The Buddha presented the twelve links in the chain of dependent origination, from the first link—fundamental ignorance—up to the twelfth link—aging and death—to describe the dependently originated nature of cyclic existence. When the mechanisms of cause and effect at the heart of the four noble truths are explained in greater detail, we arrive at the Buddha's teaching on the twelve links of dependent origination.

As with his teachings of the four noble truths, the Buddha taught two causal processes with respect to these twelve links.[6] And here too the first process pertains to the afflicted class of phenomena, while the second pertains to the enlightened class. In the afflicted process, the links proceed in their regular sequence from cause to effect, with each effect becoming in turn a cause for the next effect, culminating in the suffering of cyclic existence. In the process pertaining to enlightenment, however, the cessation of the causes leads to the cessation of the effects—first one link ceases, then another, until cyclic existence comes to an end. In other words, the first two noble truths—the truth of suffering and the truth of its origin—explain the emergence of the twelve links, while the two last truths—cessation and the path—describe the dissolution of the twelve links and the result of liberation.

All twelve of the twelve links fall into the classes of suffering and its origin. Master Nagarjuna writes in his *Exposition of the Essence of Dependent Origination:*

> The first, eighth, and ninth are afflictions;
> the second and tenth are actions;
> the remaining links are suffering.[7]

Here, Nagarjuna explains that, of the twelve links of dependent origination, the first, *ignorance,* the eighth, *craving,* and the ninth, *grasping,* are the origin of suffering in the form of afflictions, while the second, *volition,* and the tenth, *becoming,* are the origin in the form of karmic action. These five thus constitute the truth of the origin of suffering. The remaining seven—from the third, *consciousness,* through *name and form, sources, contact, feeling,* and *birth* up to the twelfth, *aging and death*—constitute the truth of suffering.

Fundamental ignorance, the first link

In chapter 26 of the *Fundamental Stanzas on the Middle Way,* Nagarjuna begins by presenting the first two links, fundamental ignorance and the volitional act:

> 1. Obscured by ignorance and for the sake of rebirth
>   we create the three kinds of action;
>   it is these actions constructing [existence]
>   that propel us through transmigration.[8]

Ignorance obscures the true nature of reality and distorts the way we apprehend objects, and on this basis, the grasping at self-existence arises. Due to the force of this ignorance, whatever objects we encounter in our sphere of experience—forms, sounds, and so on—our perceptions of them are distorted by the conceptualization of true existence. These projections engendered by a false way of attending to the objects lead to attachment and aversion, and these in turn lead to the accumulation of karma for rebirth in cyclic existence.

Under the spell of aversion or attachment, for instance, we may act in a way that harms others and thereby accumulate *demeritorious* or *unwholesome karma* and be reborn in the lower realms. On the other hand, driven by attachment, we may engage in acts of helping others and so earn *meritorious karma* and a pleasant rebirth, but the attachment means the act is still rooted in false projections arising from grasping at true existence. Then, disillusioned even by pleasure and aspiring for a state of equanimity, we may accumulate *unwavering karma* on the basis of deep meditative absorptions. The phrase "the three types of actions," then, refers to these three: (1) the demeritorious karma that propels birth in the lower realms, (2) the meritorious karma that propels birth as a human or a *deva* god in the desire realm, and (3) the unwavering karma that propels birth in the form and formless realms. The last two are both varieties of meritorious karma but create different results due to the aspiration that motivated the action.

These three types of karma are what are referred to as "that which constructs" birth in the cycle of existence. Alternatively, the "three actions" here may be identified as the karmic acts of body, speech, and mind performed under the influence of the mental poisons. It depends on the perspective you approach it from. From the perspective of their results there are the demeritorious, meritorious, and unwavering karmas, while from the standpoint of the avenues through which the deeds are committed, there are the karmic acts of body, speech, and mind. All of these karmic acts are accumulated through the force of the ignorance that fails to understand the true nature of reality.

A demeritorious act—an act in other words done in disregard of others' welfare and harmful to others—is driven by two types of ignorance. There is (1) the *causal* motivating factor, which is ignorance of the true nature of reality, and there is (2) the *coemergent* motivating factor—that which arises together with the action—which is ignorance of the law of karma. Ignorance of the law of karma is a nihilism that denies cause and effect. Ignorance in general is twofold—merely *not knowing* something and *distorted knowing*, thinking something to be true that is false. The two motivating factors of a demeritorious act are both distorted knowing. If the ignorance motivating a deed were simply not knowing something, the underlying state of mind would be neutral, neither virtuous nor nonvirtuous.

Distorted knowing, too, comes in multiple types, such as those that involve denigration—for example, the view that derides the law of karma—and those that involve reification. An example of the latter would be ignorance of the gross level of grasping at self-existence of persons and phenomena. However, if we trace the ultimate source of all the types of ignorance that involve distorted knowing, we find they are rooted in the ignorance grasping at true existence of things. This is the fundamental ignorance, the first of the twelve links. It is called *ignorance* because it distorts the perception of the true nature of reality.

To understand the way ignorance underlies unenlightened existence, we need to examine a paradox that we all experience. We all equally shun suffering and aspire for happiness, yet we still experience a great deal of suffering against our wishes and rarely find the lasting happiness we seek. These sufferings do not arise without a cause; they are produced by causes and conditions. And if we trace these causes and conditions to their ultimate sources, we will find that we have gathered them ourselves. This fact—that we create the conditions for suffering despite wishing to avoid suffering—can only persist because of ignorance. Were we not ignorant, we would not pursue the conditions for our own suffering. In short, our problems and misfortunes come about principally due to karma we create ourselves, and we do this under the power of ignorance.

The last part of this stanza "these actions...propel us through transmigration" means that our karma determines whether our birth is good or bad. As we just saw above, there are the three types of volitional acts—demeritorious, meritorious, and unwavering—which produce three corresponding types of birth. In terms of their actual nature, there is the *act of intending* itself and the *intended action*—the idea and its execution. Nagarjuna's Middle Way, or Madhyamaka, school agrees with the Vaibhashika (Great Exposition) school that the intended action is a physical one—an act of body or speech.

IMPRINTS ON OUR CONSCIOUSNESS

Returning to Nagarjuna's text:

2a–b. **With volition as its condition,**
consciousness enters transmigration.

Once the karmic act has been performed, both the action of intending and the intended act cease. Following their cessation, some imprint of the karma is left behind. Where exactly are these imprints left? Without distinguishing different levels of subtlety of the body and just taking the gross physical body, we can see that its continuum is not stable and can easily disintegrate. Thus it would be difficult to posit the body as the repository for the karmic imprints. In contrast, again without distinguishing consciousness's different levels of subtlety, consciousness—which according to Buddhism goes from life to life—is more stable than the body in terms of its continuum. Therefore, the inner consciousness is where the residues of karma are imprinted.

When we speak of imprints, we are speaking of the mental propensities created by the karma collected in the past that is stored until conditions assemble for those propensities to be released. It is imprints that connect the committing of acts in the past to the reaping of their fruits at some future time. This is why the repository of the imprints must have a stable continuum. To address this, some past Buddhist masters posited a foundational consciousness (*alayavijñana*) as the basis of the imprints. Others, believing that the essence of the person can be found when sought critically, considered the consciousness they identified as the essence of the person as the basis of the imprints. Both of these explanations create a basis for explaining how karmic imprints are carried from life to life, but they also lead to other philosophical problems. The way Nagarjuna's Madhyamaka school approaches it is different.

When Chandrakirti interpreted Nagarjuna's unique standpoints, he drew a distinction between a temporary basis of the imprints and a more enduring basis. He said that the immediate consciousness contemporaneous with the karmic act is the temporary basis of the imprint, while the enduring basis of the imprints is the I or the "person" that is constructed on the basis of the continuity of the person's consciousness.

Neither of these bases can be found when the true referents of their terms are sought through critical inquiry. They are mere conceptual constructs, albeit conventionalities not negated by some other conventionally valid cognition. However, by positing as the basis of the imprints, which are themselves real in name and concept only, the "mere I," which is also real in name and concept only, you end up with a very elegant solution. The Indian masters analyzed and reflected upon this extensively.

Here, in a very general way, I have stated that consciousness, which possesses a stable continuum, is the basis of the imprints. Chandrakirti, commenting on Nagarjuna's unique approach, provides a more sophisticated explanation. A *functioning entity* is defined by classical Indian Buddhists as something that can produce an effect. Chandrakirti, as a Madhyamika, accepts the *disintegration* or cessation of a conditioned thing as a functioning entity, in other words as causally effective, and he explains this as follows. *Disintegration* is the state of a conditioned thing that is established when the thing ceases, or comes to an end. This disintegration is produced by the very same cause that gave birth to the thing in the first place—the seed of disintegration is present in the birth of all conditioned things—and therefore the disintegration too is understood to have arisen from a cause. By definition, then, since that cessation is produced from a cause, it must itself be a cause, which is to say that it must be a functioning thing.

On this basis he claims that it is the disintegration, which is actually the cessation of the karma, that produces the fruits of the karma. This continuation of disintegrated states of karma can be conceived coherently only on the basis of the continuum of consciousness or the "mere I." No other basis makes sense.

Now, all the classical Buddhist schools below Svatantrika Madhyamaka assert that although [the act of] disintegrating is caused, disintegration itself is not caused. In the aftermath of the disintegrating, they say, you can't find any remnant of the conditioned thing that was produced by a cause. By this same logic, however, then you should also say that although arising is caused, the arisen, being already established, would have no need for a cause, and in that case, you would also say that the arisen is not produced by a cause. You could apply the same argument along these lines. In any case, the Prasangika Madhyamikas say that since the ceasing is produced by a cause, the cessation that exists in the wake of the ceasing is also produced by a cause. Using this same logic, Prasangika Madhyamikas claim that the person designated upon the basis of the stream of consciousness, having accumulated countless different karmas, will bear the continuity of the cessation of karmic acts.

The meaning of "consciousness with volition as its condition" then is this: The consciousness that is the repository of imprints is called the causal consciousness, while the consciousness that the effects from the imprint-laden consciousness ripen upon in the new birth is called the resultant consciousness. The consciousness presented here as the third link is a causal consciousness, specifically one that is the basis for the imprint of a karmic act motivated by ignorance that is capable of projecting the continuum into a new birth in cyclic existence.

Beginningless mind

The tantras speak of various levels of consciousness. This important topic requires serious contemplation. For example, because the grossest level of consciousness is heavily connected with the body—including the subtle body with its so-called channels, winds, and drops—the body becomes the support and the gross consciousness the supported. When the body, the support, dissolves, the supported gross consciousness dissolves as well. For example, when the eye organ breaks down, the visual consciousness breaks down, too.

Like this, many types of consciousness are contingent upon the body. We speak, for instance, of "human consciousness," "consciousness at the time of old age," and "consciousness of the sick," and these are each clearly contingent upon a body. You often hear Buddhists say that the mind—the continuum of consciousness—is beginningless, but they are not talking about such gross consciousnesses. Clearly, when the support—the body—comes into being, the sense organs form gradually, giving rise to the sensory perceptions. Similarly, when the body degenerates, some of the cognitive faculties contingent upon it also degenerate, such as through memory loss. Finally, when the body ceases to exist, the consciousness dependent upon it also comes to an end. This cannot be the beginningless consciousness. However, those consciousnesses that arose with the body as their support arise nonetheless in their luminous and knowing nature, and there must be a unique condition that allows them to arise in such nature. "Luminous" in this context simply means that it is non-physical, and "knowing" means that it can be aware of things. "Luminous and knowing" is the standard definition of consciousness in Buddhism.

In general, just because there is a physical organ doesn't mean there will be consciousness as well. For example, before a child's conception, the physical basis exists, but there is no supported consciousness. Conception here is not identical to fertilization; for Buddhists conception occurs when the continuum of consciousness enters the body. There is a process involved that takes time. The fertilized egg in the womb remains the same before and after conception, but prior to conception, it does not support a consciousness. Now, if the mere existence of a fertilized egg necessarily entailed the presence of a gross consciousness, regardless of the moment of conception, then there should be feeling and so on, too, whether or not conception has taken place.

The question of when exactly the consciousness enters the womb requires further investigation. Texts of both sutra and tantra name a stage when the parents' "regenerative fluids" come together and the consciousness enters, but such statements are from a broad standpoint and not necessarily definitive. Today, through technology, an egg can even be fertilized outside the womb leading to successful conception, after which the embryo is inserted into the womb. Some ancient stories also relate incidents of conception taking place outside the mother's womb. Thus human conception need not occur inside the womb.

I often bring up these issues because things like this that do not accord with the explanations in the texts can be seen today. For example, the size, distance, and so on of the sun and moon listed in Vasubandhu's *Treasury of Higher Knowledge* (*Abhidharmakosha*) contradict the measurements determined by empirical observation and mathematical calculation. To uphold the measurements in the Buddhist treatises would be a defiance of empirical evidence. Furthermore, since the Buddha said that we must reject philosophical tenets that conflict with reason, it is all the more inappropriate to uphold a tenet that defies direct experience. The same logic applies to the issue of when conception takes place. The explanations in the Buddhist treatises must be taken as broad guidelines and not as definitive, final words.

How can we determine the authenticity of scriptural references to what are called "extremely hidden" facts (as opposed to, say, knowledge of emptiness which is hidden, though can be inferred through reasoning)—things we cannot know through observation with an ordinary mind?[9] Buddhist treatises state that we can validate scriptures that pertain to extremely hidden facts by checking whether they contain any internal inconsistencies. Scriptures sometimes contradict each other—for example, Mount Meru and the four continents are central to Buddhist cosmology, but some scriptures say Mount Meru is square, and some say it is circular. Assertions like this must be verified by examining whether the scripture is free of internal contradictions.

To return to our earlier point, there must be a unique condition to enable the consciousness to arise as luminous and knowing. We speak of "human" or "becoming a human," and becoming a human happens when the consciousness arises on the basis of the parents' reproductive secretions. However, what is the condition that enables that consciousness to have the nature of luminosity and the capacity to perceive an object? A physical basis is not sufficient. Consciousness requires a prior continuum that shares its luminous and knowing identity. The human body serves as a cooperative condition for a "human consciousness," but because it is physical and not luminous, it cannot be the substantial cause of that consciousness. The main cause of consciousness must be a prior moment of consciousness.

This is why Buddhism posits past and future lives. Some individuals can even recall their past lives. By mastering the meditative absorptions, we can, on the basis of our present gross level of consciousness, enhance the capacity of our memory to such a state that remembering our previous lives becomes possible. As this capacity increases, we may even be able to intuit—in broad terms—events in the future.

In my own experience, I had indications on several occasions that Kyapjé Ling Rinpoché, one of my main mentors, possessed such superior cognition—he seemed to be able to read others' minds. One day, I asked him about it directly. Rinpoché replied that he seemed to be able to intuit things once in a while, and he did not deny possessing superior cognition. As a fully ordained monk, had Rinpoché claimed superior cognition without this being true, he would have broken his vow to abstain from false proclamations of spiritual realizations, and he would have had to disrobe! I have known others as well who, through the power of their meditative practices, have recollected their past lives. So these things do happen, although I am not sure whether they arise on the level of a subtle consciousness or by some other mechanism.

The essential point is this: The luminous and knowing aspect of a given state of consciousness must come from a prior moment of that consciousness. It follows, therefore, that it must also be beginingless. For were a beginning to the continuum of the luminous and knowing aspect of consciousness posited, we would then have to concede that the consciousness arose from a cause that is not commensurate with it, which is untenable. We see this also with material things, where every physical substance, regardless of its subtlety, has shape and color, and its substantial cause is another material substance, whose continuum we can trace back in time. This is not the effect of karma; this is simply the way the material world works. Thus, the existence of consciousness as luminous and knowing and the existence of matter as nonmental are facets of the way things naturally are. Each has its own distinct causal continuity, while at the same time, each impacts the other as a cooperative condition.

THE FOUR PRINCIPLES

Buddhist treatises speak of four avenues, or principles, of reasoning —the principle of nature, the principle of dependence, the principle of function, and the principle of evidence. Parallels of these four principles, which are like natural laws, are found in science as well. The *principle of nature* just means that the world exists in a particular way and not another way, as for instance in the above example of the mental and material continuities, and to reason based on this principle would mean to argue that phenomena must conform to the way things are. Also, by observing such properties of nature, other properties can be deduced.

Changes in the forms and states of phenomena are effected both through the interdependence of coexistent things and through the occurrence of causal sequences. This arising of different effects illustrates the *principle of dependence*, which is that everything arises from an appropriate cause. To apply this principle in rational analysis, we would argue that because so-and-so is the case, such-and-such must also be true. For example, I could infer that if anger arises in me today, it won't just disappear. It will produce some kind of effect, such as restlessness, which will in turn become a cause for yet another effect.

This relates closely to the *principle of function*, which investigates the fruits of a given phenomenon—seeing what it produces. Thus, the byproduct of an angry mind is restlessness and the byproduct of a generous mind is tranquility. Likewise, Buddhism teaches that positive actions result in pleasurable experiences and negative actions bring suffering. The seed of the result is in some sense present in its cause, just as the potential for an oak tree is present in an acorn. To reason along these lines is to make use of the principle of function.

The *principle of evidence* refers to the larger inferences that can be drawn on the basis of the first three principles. This principle is illustrated in statements such as, "If you want to find lasting happiness, you must discipline your mind." The mind exists as a continuum (the principle of nature), one moment of consciousness transforms subsequent ones (the principle of dependence), harmful intentions result in unpleasant experiences (the principle of function), therefore, if you don't want to suffer and you want to be happy, you have to learn to control your mind in order to create only positive, beneficial intentions. By reflecting on these facts, seeing how different mental states have different functions, you will come to understand deeply how disciplining the mind leads to happiness, and you will develop greater insight into the way things are.

WHY THINGS CHANGE

Since you began reading this book, some time has passed. Time, of course, never stands still; it keeps moving, moment after moment. Just as living beings, the inhabitants of the world, undergo change, so too does the world they live in, their external environment. Under what power does both the external environment and beings within it undergo change? It is because these things arose from causes in the first place. The fact that all conditioned things undergo change on a moment-by-moment basis is not the result of some third factor or outside force. The cause that produced them is by its very nature subject to change, and since things share the nature of their cause, they too are subject to change—even over the course of the briefest millisecond.

In general, we can speak of the gross level of impermanence—as when we die or when, say, something is burned or demolished. This is also called "impermanence in terms of a cessation of continued existence." This occurs upon encountering conditions adverse to the continuation of a given phenomenon. Disintegration on a moment-by-moment level is a more subtle impermanence, and it is this kind of impermanence that characterizes the various causes of phenomena. The impermanence in the Buddhist teaching that "All conditioned things are impermanent" refers to this subtle impermanence.

Now, if we investigate, we will see clearly that the notion that things can arise from no cause at all leads to all sorts of extreme consequences and contradictions. For example, there would be no reason at all then why plants could not grow in the midst of a freezing winter. In brief, if things could arise from no cause at all, this would entail a breakdown of the entire law of cause and effect and not just the breakdown of karmic causality. In contrast, the explanation that things result from causes is free from such logical fallacies.

Further, if that cause is identified to be eternal, this too is logically suspect. If the cause never changes and persists at all times, its effects, which share the same nature, would also not be subject to change. Since we can verify through our own empirical observation that an effect is subject to change, we can deduce that its main cause is subject to change as well. Not only that, the process of causation itself transforms the cause, and so for something to truly be eternal, it could not produce things, for that would change it. Thus the notion that something can arise from an eternal cause is untenable.

Similarly, the assertion that things can arise from a cause that is incommensurate with its effects is also untenable, which is to say that specific characteristics of the effect must correlate to potencies immanent in the causal stage. All the characteristics of the effect need not be present in the causal phase, but the various properties of the effects must correspond to potentialities present in the cause. Oak trees come from acorns and not from apple seeds—cause and effect must accord with each other. It is only on the basis of such a concordant relation that we can correlate phenomena as cause and effect.

It is also difficult to posit that effects arise from one single cause. Only through the aggregation of numerous causes and conditions do effects arise. There is what we might call a direct cause, but that cause's efficacy in turn depends upon many other causes and conditions, and the mere presence of that cause does not, in itself, prove that a specific effect will come to exist. Why is this? It is changes in the manifestations of the cause that allows the effects to arise, and some elements of the total causal nexus could fail to materialize prior to the arising of the effect. An acorn, for instance, might not get sufficient earth, water, or sunlight to sprout and grow. In fact, the contingencies that underlie the arising of any phenomenon are so complex and vast as to be infinite. So, except in the case of a direct cause with unstoppable potency—where the cause is ripe and its presence almost assures the existence of the effect—the presence of the cause does not guarantee the arising of the effect. Only on the basis of numerous causes and conditions do effects arise, and one single independent cause producing an effect is not possible.

Now within this network of causes and effects, there are two kinds—the network of matter and the external world and the network of the inner world of thoughts, feelings, and such. Thus we can speak of physical causality and mental causality. While the two kinds of cause and effect—material and mental—operate in their own spheres, they nonetheless affect each other. Experiences of happiness and suffering emerge in dependence upon the external material world, and in such a case we speak of an *objective condition*. For example, a mental state of fear might arise in dependence on an external object, such as a snake. But for an inner experience of happiness or suffering to arise, there must be an inner causal condition as well. The snake alone is not sufficient to induce an experience of fear. Experiences of happiness and suffering arise on the basis of these two.

One important dimension of this interface between the cause and effect of the inner (mental) world and the cause and effect interactions in the external (nonmental) world is the intention of the agent. This is where *karma* comes into the picture. It is our intention—motivations driving actions—that leaves imprints on our mind and becomes a cause for future experiences of happiness and suffering, pain and pleasure. Thus karma is part of the inner, mental network of cause and effect.

In each of the three elements of Buddhism we discussed earlier—ground, path, and result—the law of cause and effect operates. The natural law of cause and effect is an important facet of the ground—the way things are—and both the path and the final result depend on the complex mechanism of causality as well.

Karma, the second link

Actions can be pure, such as the uncontaminated actions that give rise to the enlightened qualities on the various levels of the path, or afflicted. In the context of the twelve links, the actions or karma being referred to is the unenlightened afflicted class of karma that projects us into continued rebirth within the cycle of existence. The seed of this karma is rooted in the afflictions, with fundamental ignorance as the root affliction, and these lead to the effects all the way up to aging and death. As Nagarjuna stated in verse 1, "Obscured by ignorance and for the sake of rebirth, we create the three kinds of action." In other words, by means of the karmic act accumulated through the power of fundamental ignorance, a *projecting karma* is formed—a karma that propels a new rebirth in samsara.

Karmic acts are all rooted in ignorance, but they are not all equal. As long as we have not attained the "path of seeing," the point at which the obscuration of fundamental ignorance has been fully penetrated by means of a direct realization of emptiness, all our actions will be contaminated by that ignorance. But some karmic actions—specifically, actions tempered by the correct view of emptiness, true renunciation, and the awakening mind—can help lead us out of ignorance, and these do not constitute the second link. Karmic acts formed on the basis of true knowledge—seeing everything as illusion-like, devoid of true existence—are utterly different from the karmic acts that project birth in samsaric existence. The same is true for actions driven by true renunciation—such as the heartfelt thought "How I wish to be free from existence conditioned by suffering!" that arises upon recognizing that the afflictions are what chain us to suffering. And it is true as well for acts accumulated through the awakening mind, the altruistic intention to secure the welfare of all sentient beings. Actions such as these constitute only a similitude of the truth of the origin of suffering, and their fruits ripen as the conditions for spiritual practice. For example, the attainment through positive karma of the unique bodily existence as a human being in the fortunate realm, which is the basis for cultivating omniscience, can also be a byproduct of generating the awakening mind.

In brief, the second link, volitional action, is a karmic act accumulated with fundamental ignorance as its causal motivation that produces samsaric existence. In contrast, acts accumulated on the basis of recognizing everything as devoid of true existence, or acts tempered by genuine renunciation or by an uncontrived awakening mind, constitute conditions for attaining the definite goodness. Just as I always state that whether an act is karmically wholesome or unwholesome depends on its underlying motivation, in the same way, whether an act produces samsaric existence or leads to liberation is principally determined by the underlying motivation.

The state of our minds as we approach death is very important from the Buddhist perspective. You could say that our state of mind at the time of death steers the course of our next rebirth. If the activating factors are craving and grasping, these steer the karmic course in one direction. However, if the activating factor is compassion or altruism, that will steer us in another direction.

There is a story from Gungthang Rinpoché's time at Tashikhyil Monastery.[10] An old monk on the verge of death clung to his life for such a long time that Gungthang Rinpoché came to see him to determine what was happening. What he discovered was that the monk was deeply attached to Tashikhyil Monastery's delicious butter tea. Gungthang Rinpoché reassured the elderly monk: "Don't worry. In

Tushita heaven, the butter tea is even better!" As a result, the monk was apparently able to let go and pass away peacefully. So the question here is, which karmic factor was activated at the time of his death—his attachment to tea or his wish to be born in Tushita!

Even ordinary people like us, whose minds are dominated by delusions and ignorance, can propel rebirth through the force of mental states like compassion and altruistic aspiration. It is vital, especially for practicing Buddhists, to make our state of mind at the time of death virtuous. It's important for the dying individual, and for the people around the dying person it's also important to create an atmosphere that will encourage the dying person to develop a virtuous state of mind.

THE THIRD AND FOURTH LINKS

Nagarjuna goes on to say,

> **2c–d. Once consciousness has entered,**
> **name and form come to be.**

The third link is *consciousness,* specifically the consciousness inscribed with the imprints of such volitional acts that will launch a new birth. Four general types of rebirth are mentioned in Maitreya's *Ornament of Mahayana Sutras* (*Mahayanasutralamkara*).¹¹ There is rebirth propelled by karma and afflictions—i.e., through the completion of the tenth of the twelve links of dependent origination, namely *becoming.* There is rebirth propelled by compassion; there is rebirth propelled by prayers of aspiration; and there is rebirth propelled by meditative absorptions. So rebirth can occur in different ways.

In any case, don't think of consciousness here as a discrete entity that exists on its own. Consciousness always depends upon a basis. In the treatises of the sutra system, consciousness is explained on the basis of the gross physical body. In highest yoga tantra, which identifies gross, subtle, and extremely subtle levels of mind, the body is similarly said to have gross, subtle, and extremely subtle levels, which act as bases for the three levels of mind. In all cases, regardless of its subtlety, consciousness depends on a body. Thus at death, when the gross body is discarded, the extremely subtle body remains inseparable with consciousness. The I that is designated upon this extremely subtle body, too, continues to exist inseparably.

To take the example of a womb-born being in the desire realm, the sensory bases begin to form when consciousness connects with the new birth. At that time, when the new gross bodily existence is first beginning, all five aggregates already exist there. Therefore, in the line "Name and form come to be," the gross body is referred to as "form," and the remaining four nonphysical aggregates—feeling, discrimination, mental formations, and conscious awareness—are given the label "name." *Name and form* is the fourth of the twelve links of dependent origination.

THE FIFTH, SIXTH, AND SEVENTH LINKS

Nagarjuna then continues with:

> 3a–b. Once name and form have developed,
> The six sense spheres come into being.

After the name-and-form link materializes, there emerges—during the first, second, and the third weeks of human gestation—the six sense spheres or "sources" (*ayatana*): the eye organ, ear organ, nose organ, tongue organ, body organ, and mental organ. This group of six sense spheres is the fifth link in the chain of dependent origination. The sense spheres are subtle material organs or faculties—rather than the gross physical organs *per se*—and they act as intermediaries between the six types of sense objects on the one hand and the six sensory consciousnesses that cognize them on the other. The six sense faculties are said to be the "dominant condition" for sense cognitions to arise.

> 3c–d. Depending on the six sense spheres,
>   contact comes into being;

> 4. It arises only in dependence
>   on eye, form, and apprehension;
>   thus, in dependence on name and form,
>   consciousness arises.

> 5a–c. The convergence of the three—
>   eye, form, and consciousness—
>   this is contact....

Buddhist treatises appear to indicate that the body's tactile sense faculty exists even in the womb, when the body consciousness comes into contact with body's tactile aspect. Similarly, I think the ear consciousness hears sound then as well. As for the nose consciousness cognizing smell or the tongue consciousness cognizing taste, I do not know, and there is no contact yet between the eye consciousness and visual objects. Nonetheless, the sense organs—the eye faculty and so on—are already formed in the womb. After birth, it is the coming together of three factors—in the case of a visual experience, an external form, the eye sensory faculty that is the dominant condition, and the visual consciousness—that allows cognitions apprehending their corresponding objects to arise. The other types of sensory cognitions are described similarly. It is this coming together of object, sensory faculty, and consciousness that is referred to as *contact*.

> 5c–d. ...From contact
> feeling comes into being.

Feeling here does not refer to our complex emotions of anger, jealousy, and the like, so much as whether we experience something as pleasant, unpleasant, or neutral. Once contact occurs—the convergence of object, sense faculty, and consciousness—then as part of a causal chain that perpetuates cyclic existence, contact leads to either pleasurable or disagreeable feelings or experiences, the seventh link.

Eighth and ninth links

Nagarjuna continues:

> 6a–b. Conditioned by feeling is craving;
> one craves because of feeling;

The feelings that arise on the basis of contact are tainted by the projection of true existence onto things. These feelings, in turn, produce two kinds of craving—craving pleasurable sensations, in the sense of not wanting to be separated from them, and craving separation from painful feelings. It is on the basis of these two types of craving (the eighth link) that attachment and aversion arise.

> **6c–d. When one craves, there is grasping;**
> **the four kinds of grasping [take place].**

Here *grasping*, or *appropriation*, is a form of attachment. As we just saw, conditioned by feeling, craving arises in the form of wanting desirable sensation and wanting separation from undesirable sensation. For the sake of these sensations, one develops attachment to the sensory objects, to one's views, or to a false morality that is based on ignorance. One thus develops the four forms of grasping—grasping at sensory objects, at views, at self-righteousness, and at the deluded view of a self. These four are referred to as "appropriation" because one appropriates them out of the conviction that they lead to pleasurable feelings. They do not. This misperception, and the appropriation it entails, keeps the engine of cyclic existence running.

In short, the aggregates are the basis for obtaining negative states of existence, and when the aggregates meet the appropriate circumstances, contact and feeling arise; in dependence upon these, craving arises, and from craving arises grasping, or appropriation, the ninth link.

The tenth, eleventh, and twelfth links

Nagarjuna goes on to say

> 7. Where there is grasping,
>   the becoming of the grasper thoroughly comes to be.
>   Were there no grasping, then,
>   being free, there would be no becoming.

The second link, the volitional karmic act, ceases the moment the act has been committed. As for the tenth link, *becoming,* one understands this either, as explained earlier, in terms of the disintegration of the karmic act or in terms of the potency of that karma. In any case, becoming, or *existence,* is the karmic seed now activated by craving and appropriation and thus transformed into a potent capacity certain to bring its karmic effect. This belongs in the category of karma, or cause, but since it is the state of the karma that immediately precedes the effect, namely a new existence, it is being referred to by the name of its effect. It is the stage in the continuum of a karmic seed where its potency has come to full maturity and the effect is imminent.

> 8a–b. This becoming is also the five aggregates,
>   and from becoming emerges birth.

Karmic actions, as we've seen, are created through body, speech, and mind. Of these three types of actions, those of body and speech belong to form aggregate, while mental acts belong to the other four aggregates—feeling, discrimination, mental formations, and conscious awareness. Becoming or existence is their fruit, and it is from such becoming that birth, the eleventh link, comes into being.

Buddhist scriptures speak of four types of birth—womb, egg, heat and moisture, and spontaneous. Of these, the first two are commonly observed, while birth from heat and moisture requires more investigation. A spontaneous birth is a birth where all the sense faculties emerge simultaneously in a mature form. The reference to birth in the line "And from becoming emerges birth" is, I believe, made from the point of view of birth from a womb. In a womb birth, the first moment of this link is the moment of conception, when the consciousness enters the fertilized egg.

> 8c–d.   Aging, death, and sorrow,
>   grief, suffering, and so on,

> 9a–b.   As well as unhappiness and agitation:
>   these come from birth.

After the link of birth arises the link of aging, where the physical and mental aggregates mature and transform through various stages. The second part of the twelfth link, death, arises where even the type-continuum of the aggregates (which is to say, their continuum as the psychophysical constituents of the being) comes to be discarded. Furthermore, even when alive, we mentally experience suffering, verbally utter lamentations, and bodily undergo pain. Alternatively, the lines can be read as stating that in dependence upon birth, we experience sorrow in general and the uttering of lamentations in particular; the physical pain, mental unhappiness, and disturbances will thoroughly ensue.

9c–d. What comes into being
  is only a mass of suffering.

Nagarjuna here speaks of a "mass of suffering." This expression is found in a sutra on dependent origination,[12] and I believe Nagarjuna is using this expression here in the same manner. This collection of aggregates—which has fundamental ignorance as its cause and attachment and aversion as its cooperative conditions—is subject to suffering from the moment of birth until the close of life. Furthermore, since it is the vehicle for creating more suffering in future lives, we are perpetually denied the happiness we long for, and we continue to suffer the torment we do not want. In this way beings are trapped in a wheel of samsaric existence, which is therefore called "the mass of suffering." Of the three kinds of suffering—evident suffering, changeable suffering, and the suffering of conditioning (as explored in the first chapter)—the suffering in the Buddha's expression "the mass of suffering" is primarily the suffering of conditioning.

THE TWELVE LINKS IN REVERSE SEQUENCE

Nagarjuna then begins to present the twelve links in reverse sequence:

10. The root of cyclic existence is action;
  therefore, the wise do not act.
  The unwise one is an agent;
  the wise one, seeing suchness, is not.

By stating how the wise person, by not engaging in karmic acts (i.e., acts contaminated by ignorance), does not perpetuate the cycle of existence, this verse suggests the explanation of the reverse sequence of the twelve links of dependent origination. Having studied the sequence of origination from ignorance to aging and death, we might wonder what is the root of this burden we carry, the collection of aggregates, which continuously mires us in misfortune? It is all due to having taken *birth* within the aggregates assumed through karma and afflictions. We do not assume the aggregates out of our freedom and choice; we are obligated by the dictates of the cause of our aggregates—the link of *becoming*. The link of becoming need only be established within our mental continuum, and we have no choice but to take rebirth. The establishment of the link of *becoming* rests, in turn, on the activation of our karma through *craving* and *appropriation* or *grasping*. The formation of craving and appropriation, likewise, requires our grasping at the true existence of our pleasant or unpleasant *feelings*. The arising of such feelings, in turn, is predicated on encountering desirable, undesirable, or neutral objects. This is *contact*, the convergence of object, sensory faculty, and consciousness. Such contact, in turn, requires the full presence of the *six sense spheres*, which, in turn, depend upon *name and form*—in other words, the five psychophysical aggregates.

When the link of name and form is propelled by *ignorance*, it becomes the basis of suffering. However, when name and form are propelled by such factors as the awakening mind that takes others to be more precious than oneself, they probably will not become a basis for suffering. Therefore, for name and form to constitute the fourth link, they must be propelled by causes that produce suffering.

The links beginning with name and form are called the *propelled effects,* and the arising of name and form requires the presence of a *propelling cause.* What are these propelling causes? The Buddha identified the first three links as propelling causes—the third, *consciousness,* the second, *volitional action,* and the first, *ignorance.* In brief, name-and-form comes into being based on the consciousness inscribed with karmic imprints; and for that consciousness to arise, action engendered by ignorance—either positive or negative karma—must be accumulated. That ignorance could be ignorance of the law of karma in the immediate term, but the ultimate cause or root ignorance is the delusion that grasps at true existence.

This is why, when the reason for explaining the twelve links of dependent origination is given, the root is traced back to ignorance. For example, when Aryadeva states in the following that "consciousness" is the seed of cyclic existence, he is primarily thinking of ignorance as the core of that consciousness:

> Consciousness is the seed of existence,
> while objects are its field of experience.
> When, with respect to objects, no self is seen,
> the seed of existence will cease.[13]

HOW THE TWELVE LINKS OF DEPENDENT ORIGINATION ARE COMPLETED

A cycle of twelve links of dependent origination has a beginning and an ending. For a single cycle, we can understand this as follows.

Right now we are experiencing the effect of a volitional act that was accumulated on the basis of a specific instance of ignorance, a karma that propelled this embodied existence. Thus we are amid a cycle of twelve links that began with the ignorance that propelled our current existence and will continue until the link of aging and death comes to fruition. From the time we woke up this morning until the present moment, the thought "I am" has arisen constantly. This arises on the basis of perceiving the aggregates as truly existent and clinging to them as such. Thus, in our everyday lives, there are countless instances where the perception of and clinging to our physical and mental aggregates as possessing true existence serves as the basis for the arising of grasping I and "I am."

In exceptional cases, where people have developed a powerful understanding of no-self, when the thought "I am" arises, they recall that the I does not actually exist. Similarly, when they encounter external objects—forms, sounds, and so on—they recognize that these do not exist in the way they appear to the mind. For most of us, however, this is difficult. Without a cultivated familiarity with the view of emptiness, the thought may occasionally occur to us that "Things are devoid of intrinsic existence," but it is not possible to recall this in every moment, and certainly not to live out its full implications.

For us, from the moment we open our eyes in the morning until the current moment, we experience afflictions because of our grasping at self-existence. Grasping at the self-existence of phenomena is the basis for the afflictions, and grasping at the self-existence of "me" is the catalyst. These afflictions may be gross ones, such as attachment and aversion, but just as likely, they are more subtle. Driven by these afflictions, we engage in all sorts of activities with body and mind.

In brief, before a single cycle of dependent origination can be completed—even within a mere moment of time—ignorance initiates so many new karmic cycles by planting imprints upon our consciousness. Therefore, the amount of volitional karma—the second link—that we have accrued through ignorance and imprinted upon our consciousness is beyond calculation. From among this vast store of karmic imprints that are ready to bring about the link of *becoming* upon meeting the necessary conditions, one is activated at the approach of death by craving and appropriation, the eighth and ninth links. In this way, when the link of *becoming* arises, the effects of the three propelling links—ignorance, karma, and consciousness—are said to come to fruition.

So, although we speak of the beginning and end of a single cycle of twelve links, in general, within the aging and death of a single cycle as well as between the contact and feeling of a single cycle, we accumulate much new karma out of ignorance. Furthermore, since grasping at an "I" remains so pervasive we can surmise by extension that afflictions such as attachment and aversion arise in the infant as well. Therefore, from our time in the womb until now, we have continually created new karma.

Thinking along the lines described above allows you to recognize that it is this ignorance, the delusion grasping at true existence, that is your true, unambiguous enemy. If, instead of endorsing the view of this delusion, you challenge it on the basis of contemplating emptiness, a genuine effect on your mind can come about. It is important to remember, in any case, that although this delusion grasping at true existence is powerful, it is nonetheless a mental state that is distorted, and a powerful antidote to it exists. If you contemplate in this manner, there is real cause for hope. Otherwise, the situation remains quite hopeless, and when you reflect upon Jé Tsongkhapa's *Three Principal Aspects of the Path*, where he says that

"They are trapped within the iron mesh of self-grasping; They are enveloped by thick mists of ignorance,"[14] you will despair and sigh in anguish.

The basis for genuine hope is encapsulated in the following lines from *Fundamental Stanzas on the Middle Way* and *Four Hundred Stanzas on the Middle Way*:

> Whatever is dependently originated,
> this is explained to be emptiness.[15]

And:

> Merely arousing a doubt about this [emptiness] teaching
> tears cyclic existence to pieces.[16]

In brief, contemplating the way we revolve in the cycle of existence through the twelve links makes us recognize that samsaric existence is limitless and that the real enemy—the root cause of our downfall—is the delusion referred to as fundamental ignorance.

Without the view of emptiness, even activities like reciting mantras for the sake of longevity and good health cause us to continue revolving in the cycle of existence. Similarly, virtuous deeds performed out of a wish for birth in a fortunate realm in our next life remain an origin of suffering and a cause for cyclic existence. No such action can be the cause for attaining liberation or omniscience. Even meditation practices, when motivated by a wish for fortunate rebirth, are causes for continued cyclic existence. As Jé Tsongkhapa writes in his *Great Treatise on the Stages of the Path*, "your virtuous activities—with some exceptions on account of the field's power—would constitute typical origins of suffering, and hence would fuel the process of cyclic existence."[17]

That is why we read in Nagarjuna's *Fundamental Stanzas on the Middle Way,*

> The unwise one is an agent;
> The wise one, seeing suchness, is not.

Nagarjuna distinguishes between the wise and the unwise based on whether the person has seen or not seen the suchness of dependent origination. Ordinary, naïve beings who lack the antidote to fundamental ignorance, an antidote worthy of confidence, are agents of the karma that propels their birth in the perpetual cycle of existence.

The text goes on to explain the need for the cessation of ignorance:

> 11a–b. When ignorance has ceased,
> actions will not arise.

To answer the question, "How can this ignorance be brought to an end?" the text states:

> 11c–d. Ignorance ceases through
> insight into and meditation on suchness.

We cannot bring about the cessation of ignorance through meditating on loving-kindness and compassion. Nor can we eliminate ignorance through meditating on the conventional awakening mind.

As these lines state, we must arrive at the decisive understanding that the true existence to which our ignorance clings does not exist at all. Understanding derived from hearing, reflection, and meditation focused on emptiness—negating true existence through analysis—this alone is not sufficient. We must also realize the correct ascertainment of emptiness within our direct experience. This is the meaning of the verses cited above.

THE SEQUENCE OF CESSATION

Next, Nagarjuna's text presents the sequence in which the twelve links of dependent origination come to cease. It reads:

> 12. Through the cessation of this and that
>   this and that do not manifest;
>   in this way the entire mass of suffering
>   ceases completely.

The meaning here is that when the first link, ignorance, ceases, the volitional act and the consciousness upon which the karmic imprint is left also cease, that is, they do not arise. In general, however, a continuity of consciousness remains in the absence of ignorance and volitional acts. Such consciousness, in itself neutral, can now serve as the basis for pure imprints, just as a piece of white cloth can be dyed either black or red.

How many lives does it take to exhaust a single cycle of the twelve links? If fast, it happens in two lives, and if slow it takes three. Here's why: In one life the person accumulates the volitional act motivated by ignorance. This volitional karma, once imprinted upon consciousness, may be activated in that very same life by craving and appropriation, so that the tenth link, becoming, comes into being. Immediately afterward in the next life, due to the link of becoming, the link of birth arises simultaneous with the link of name-and-form. This is then followed by the remaining links, including the six sense spheres, contact, feeling, and aging and death. When they arise in this above manner, the twelve links occur over two lives. It doesn't often happen, however, that the ignorant act imprinted upon the causal consciousness comes to fruition as the link of becoming within the same lifetime. Frequently, this process is interrupted, and only in some future life does that imprint encounter the conditions necessary to activate the karma through craving and appropriation; only then does the link of becoming arise. Then, immediately following the completion of the link of becoming in the second lifetime, the remaining links, from birth up to aging and death, are completed in a third lifetime. This is how a cycle of the twelve links occurs over the course of three lives.

The scriptures distinguish three types of karma based on how their effects are experienced. First, there is the *karma that one will experience here and now*—karma created in an earlier part of life whose effects are reaped later in the same life.[18] In the example where the twelve links are exhausted in two lives, the volitional act that is part of this cycle is referred to as *karma that one will experience in the next rebirth*. Finally, the volitional act in the context of the completion of the twelve links in three lives is called *karma that one will experience at other times*.

3. The Analysis of Self and No-Self

The teaching on the twelve links of dependent origination is common to all the Buddhist traditions; however, the interpretation of the twelve links, their processes, and particularly the explanation of the first link, ignorance, is different for the Madhyamaka school than it is for the other philosophical schools.

The other schools define fundamental ignorance as grasping at the self-existence of the person. Grasping at the self-existence of a person means believing there is a self that is somehow distinct from our body and mind—our aggregates. Such a self is thought to act like a master over the physical and mental components of a person.

The seventh-century Indian Buddhist philospher Dharmakirti gives an example of this belief in his *Exposition of Valid Cognition* (*Pramanavarttika*): Say an old person whose body is deteriorating and is full of aches is given the opportunity to exchange his body for another much healthier body. From the depths of his mind would emerge a ready willingness to take part in such an exchange. This suggests that deep down, we believe in a self that is distinct from our body yet is somehow master over it.

Similarly, if a person with a poor memory or some other mental deficiency were given an opportunity to exchange his or her mind for a fresh one with superior cognitive powers, again from the depth of the heart would arise a real willingness to enter into the transaction. This suggests that not only in relation to our body but also in relation to our mental faculties, we believe in a self who would benefit from such an exchange, a self that it is somehow the ruler or master of the body and mind.

The other schools define grasping at self-existence as the belief in this kind of discrete self—a self-sufficient and substantially real master that is in charge of the servant body-and-mind. For them, the negation of that kind of self is the full meaning of *selflessness*, or *no-self*. When we search for such a self by investigating whether it is separate from or identical to the psychophysical aggregates, we discover that no such self exists. The other schools' interpretation of the twelve links of dependent origination therefore defines fundamental ignorance as grasping at such a self-sufficient and substantially real self.

Madhyamikas would agree that gaining insight into such a selflessness does open the way to reversing the cycle. However, as Nagarjuna argues, while this is a form of grasping at selfhood, it does not get at the subtlest meaning of selflessness. With insight into this grosser type of selflessness, you can reverse some habits related to the grosser afflictions. But wherever there is grasping at an intrinsic existence of the aggregates—the body and mind—grasping onto a self or I based on those aggregates will always be a danger. As Nagarjuna writes in his *Precious Garland* (*Ratnavali*):

> As long as there is grasping at the aggregates,
> there is grasping at self;
> when there is grasping at self there is karma,
> and from it comes birth.[19]

Nagarjuna argues that just as grasping at the intrinsic existence of the *person* or *self* is fundamental ignorance, grasping at the intrinsic existence of the *aggregates* is also grasping at self-existence. Madhyamikas therefore distinguish two kinds of emptiness—the lack of any self that is separate from the aggregates, which they call the *emptiness of self,* and the lack of intrinsic existence of the aggregates themselves—and by extension all phenomena—which they call the *emptiness of phenomena.*[20] Realizing the first kind of emptiness, Nagarjuna and his followers argue, may temporarily suppress manifest afflictions, but it can never eradicate the subtle grasping at the true existence of things. To understand the meaning of the first link, fundamental ignorance, in its subtlest sense, we must identify and understand it as grasping at the intrinsic existence of all phenomena—including the aggregates, sense spheres, and all external objects—and not merely our sense of *I.*

THE RELATIVE I

The search for the nature of the self, the I that naturally does not desire suffering and naturally wishes to attain happiness, may have begun, in India, around three thousand years ago, if not earlier. Throughout human history people have empirically observed that certain types of strong, powerful emotions—such as hatred and extreme attachment—create problems. Hatred in fact arises out of attachment—attachment, for example, to one's own family members, community, or self. Extreme attachment creates anger or hatred when these things are threatened. Anger then leads to all kinds of conflict and battles. Some human beings have stepped back, observed, and inquired into the role of these emotions, their function, their value, and their effects.

We can discuss powerful emotions such as attachment or anger in and of themselves, but these cannot actually be comprehended in isolation from their being experienced by an individual. There is no conceiving an emotion except as an experience of some being. In fact, we cannot even separate the *objects* of attachment, anger, or hatred from the individual who conceives of them as such because the characterization does not reside in the object. One person's friend is another person's enemy. So when we speak of these emotions and particularly their objects, we cannot make objective determinations, independent of relationships.

Just as we can speak of someone being a mother, a daughter, or a spouse, only in relation to another person, likewise the objects of attachment or anger are only desirable or hateful in relation to the perceiver who is experiencing attachment or anger. All of these—mother and daughter, enemy and friend—are relative terms. The point is that emotions need a frame of reference, an "I" or self that experiences them, before we can understand the dynamics of these emotions.

A reflective person will of course then ask: what exactly is the nature of the individual, the self? And once raised, this question leads to another: Where is this self? Where could it exist? We take for granted terms like east, west, north, and south, but if we examine carefully, we see these again are relative terms that have meaning only in relation to something else. Often, that point of reference turns out to be wherever you are. One could argue, in fact, that in the Buddhist worldview, the center of cyclic existence is basically where you are. Thus, in a certain sense, you yourself are the center of the universe!

Not only that, but for each person, we ourselves are the most precious thing, and we are constantly engaged in ensuring the well-being of this most precious thing. In one sense, our business on earth is to take care of that precious inner core. In any case, this is how we tend to relate to the world and others. We create a universe with ourselves in the center, and from this point of reference, we relate to the rest of the world. With this understanding, it becomes more crucial to ask what that self is. What exactly is it?

Buddhists speak of samsara and nirvana—cyclic existence and its transcendence. The former, as we have seen, can be defined as ignorance of the ultimate nature of reality and the latter as knowledge of or insight into the ultimate nature of reality. So long as we remain ignorant of the ultimate nature of reality, we are in samsara. Once we gain insight into the ultimate nature of reality, we move toward nirvana, or the transcendence of unenlightened existence. They are differentiated on the basis of knowledge. But here again, we cannot speak of knowledge without speaking of an individual who has or does not have knowledge. We come back again to the question of the self. What exactly is its nature?

This type of inquiry predates the Buddha. Such questioning was already prevalent in India before the Buddha arrived. Until he taught, the dominant belief was that since everyone has an innate sense of selfhood, a natural instinctive notion of "I am," there must be some enduring thing that is the real self. Since the physical and mental faculties that constitute our existence are transient—they change, age, and then one day cease—they cannot be the true self. Were they the real self, then our intuition of an enduring self that is somehow independent but also a master of our body and mind would have to be false. Thus, before the Buddha, the concept of the self as independent, separate from the physical and the mental faculties, was commonly accepted.

Innate grasping of selfhood is reinforced by this kind of philosophical reflection. These Indian philosophers maintained that the self did not undergo a process of change. We say "when I was young, I was like this," and "when I am older, I will do this," and these philosophers asserted that these statements presume the presence of an unchanging entity that constitutes our identity throughout the different stages of our life.

These thinkers also maintained that since highly advanced meditators could recall their past lives, this supported their position that the self takes rebirth, moving from one life to the next. They maintained that this true self was unchanging and eternal and, somehow, independent of the physical and the mental aggregates. That was largely the consensus before the Buddha.

The Buddha argued against this position. Not only is our intuition of an inborn self a delusion, he said, but also the philosophical tenets that strengthen and reinforce such a belief are a source of all kinds of false views. The Buddhist sutras therefore refer to the belief in selfhood as itself the mind of the deceiver Mara—the embodiment of delusion—and as the source of all problems. The Buddha rejected the idea of a self that is somehow independent of the body and mind.

Does that mean then that the person does not, in any sense whatsoever, exist at all? Buddha responded that the person does indeed exist, but only in relation to and in dependence on the physical and mental aggregates. Thus the existence of the individual is accepted only as a dependent entity and not as an independent, absolute reality.

Buddhist philosophical schools therefore all agree that an independent self, separate from the body and mind, cannot be found.

What exactly is the true referent of the person, however, as when we say "I do this" or "I do that"? What exactly is the person then? It is regarding the exact identification of the nature of this dependent person that diverse opinions arose among the Buddhist schools. Given their shared acceptance of existence across lifetimes, all Buddhist philosophical schools rule out the continuum of the body as constituting the continuity of the person. Therefore, the differences of opinion surround the way the continuum of consciousness could be the basis for locating the person or the individual.

In a passage in his *Precious Garland,* Nagarjuna dissects the concept of a person and its identity by explaining that a person is not the earth element, water element, fire element, wind element, space, or consciousness. And apart from these, he asks, what else could a person be? To this he responds that a person exists as the convergence of these six constituents.[21] The term "convergence" is the crucial word, as it suggests the interaction of the constituents in mutual interdependence.

How do we understand the concept of dependence? It is helpful to reflect on a statement by Chandrakirti in his commentary on Nagarjuna's *Fundamental Stanzas on the Middle Way,* where the following explicit explanation of how to understand a buddha in terms of dependent origination is found. He writes, "What is it then? We posit the tathagata in dependence upon the aggregates, for it cannot be asserted to be either identical with or separate from the aggregates."[22] His point is that if we search for the essence of something believing we can pinpoint some real thing—something objectively real from its own side that exists as a valid referent of the term or concept—then we will fail to find anything at all.

TIME AND THE SELF

In our day-to-day interactions, we often speak of time. We all take for granted the reality of time. Were we to search for what exactly time is, we could do so in two ways. One is to search with the belief that we should be able to find something objectively real that we can define as *time*. But we immediately run into a problem. We find that time can only be understood on the basis of something else, in relation to a particular phenomenon or event. The other way to search is in a relative framework, not presuming an objectively real entity.

Take, for example, the present moment. If we search for the present moment believing that we should be able to find a unique entity in the temporal process, an objective "present," we won't find anything. As we dissect the temporal process, we instead discover that events are either past or yet to occur; we find only the past and future. Nothing is truly present because the very process of searching for it is itself a temporal process, which means that it is necessarily always at a remove from *now*.

If, on the other hand, we search for the present within the relative framework of everyday convention, we can maintain the concept of the present. We can say "this present year," for example, within the broader context of many years. Within the framework of twelve months, we can speak of "the present month." Similarly, within that month, we can speak "the present week," and so on, and in this relative context we can maintain coherently the notion of a present moment. But if we search for a real present that is present intrinsically, we cannot find it.

In just the same way, we can ascertain the existence of a person within the conventional, relative framework without needing to search for some kind of objective, intrinsically real person that is the self. We can maintain our commonsense notion of the person or individual in relation to the physical and the mental faculties that comprise our particular existence.

Because of this, we find in Nagarjuna's text references to things and events or phenomena existing only as labels or within the framework of language and designation. Of the two possible modes of existence—objectively real existence and nominal existence—objectively real existence is untenable, as we have seen. Hence we can only speak of a self conventionally or nominally—in the framework of language and consensual reality. In brief, all phenomena exist merely in dependence upon their name, through the power of worldly convention. Since they do not exist objectively, phenomena are referred to in the texts as "mere terms," "mere conceptual constructs," and "mere conventions."

SEARCHING FOR THE SELF

At the beginning of his eighteenth chapter, Nagarjuna writes:

1. If self were the aggregates,
   it would have arising and disintegration;
   if it were different from the aggregates,
   it would not have the characteristics of the aggregates.

If we are searching for an essential self that is objectively and intrinsically real, we must determine whether such a self is identical to the aggregates or is something separate from them. If the self were identical with the aggregates, then like the aggregates, the self would be subject to arising and disintegrating. If the body undergoes surgery or injury, for example, the self would also be cut or harmed. If, on the other hand, the self were totally independent of the aggregates, we could not explain any changes in the self based on changes in the aggregates, such as when an individual is first young and then old, first sick and then healthy.

Nagarjuna is in addition saying that if the self and the aggregates were entirely distinct, then we could not account for the arising of grasping at the notion of self on the basis of the aggregates. For instance, if our body were threatened, we would not experience strong grasping at self as a result. The body by nature is an impermanent phenomenon, always changing, while our notion of the self is that it is somehow changeless, and we would never confuse the two if they were indeed separate.

Thus, neither outside the aggregates nor within the aggregates can we find any tangible or real thing at all that we can call "self." Nagarjuna then writes:

> 2a–b.   If the self itself does not exist,
>   how can there be "mine"?

"Mine" is a characteristic of the self, for the thought "I am" immediately gives rise to the thought "mine." The grasping at mine is a form of grasping at selfhood because "mine" grasps at objects related to the self. It is a variation on the egoistic view, which sees everything in relation to an intrinsically existent "I." In fact, if we examine the way we perceive the world around us, we cannot speak of good and bad, or samsara and nirvana, without thinking from the perspective of an "I." We cannot speak of anything at all. Once the self becomes untenable, then our whole understanding of a world based on distinguishing self from others, mine from not mine, falls apart. Therefore, Nagarjuna writes:

> 2c–d.   Since self and mine are pacified,
>   one does not grasp at "I" and "mine."

Because the self and the mine cease, the grasping at them also does not arise. This resonates with a passage in Aryadeva's *Four Hundred Stanzas on the Middle Way* (*Chatuhshatakashastrakarika*) in which he says that when you no longer see a self in relation to an object, then the root of cyclic existence will come to an end.[23]

> 3.   One who does not grasp at "I" and "mine,"
>   that one too does not exist,
>   for the one who does not grasp
>   at "I" and "mine" does not perceive him.

In other words, the yogi who has brought an end to grasping at "I" and "mine" is him- or herself not intrinsically real. If you believe in the intrinsic reality of such a yogi, then you also grasp at selfhood. What appears to the mind of the person who has ascertained the absence of self and its properties is only the absence of all conceptual elaborations. Just as grasping at me and mine must cease, so must grasping at a yogi who has ended such grasping. Both are devoid of intrinsic existence.

The point is that our understanding of emptiness should not remain partial, such that we negate the intrinsic existence of some things but not of others. We need to develop a profound understanding of emptiness so that our perception of the lack of intrinsic existence encompasses the entire spectrum of reality and becomes totally free of any conceptual elaboration whatsoever. The understanding is one of mere absence, a simple negation of intrinsic existence.

DISMANTLING THE CAUSES OF CYCLIC EXISTENCE

Nagarjuna continues,

> 4. When thoughts of "I" and "mine" are extinguished
>   with respect to the inner and the outer,
>   the process of appropriation ceases;
>   this having ceased, birth ceases.

This refers to the twelve links of dependent origination that we already discussed. "Inner" and "outer" here can be understood as the conception of self as either among or apart from the aggregates. When grasping at self and mine ceases, then because no more karmic potentials related to external or internal phenomena are activated, the ninth link in the twelve links of dependent origination—grasping, or appropriation—will not occur. We will no longer grasp at objects of enjoyment and turn away from things we deem unattractive. Thus, although we may continue to possess karmic potentials, they are no longer activated by craving and grasping, and when this happens, birth in cyclic existence, the eleventh link, can no longer occur. This is the sense in which birth will come to an end.

Therefore, as we deepen our understanding of emptiness, the potency of our karma to propel rebirth in cyclic existence is undermined. When we realize emptiness directly, as it is stated in *Exposition of Valid Cognition*, "For he who sees the truth, no projecting exists."[24] In other words, once we gain a direct realization of emptiness, we no longer accumulate karma to propel rebirth in cyclic existence. As we gradually deepen our direct realization, so that it permeates our entire experience and destroys the afflictions, we eventually eliminate the root of grasping at intrinsic existence altogether and the continuity of rebirth in cyclic existence is cut. This is true freedom, or liberation, where we no longer create new karma through ignorance, where no conditions exist to activate past karma, and where the afflictions have been destroyed at their root. Therefore Nagarjuna writes that:

5. Karma and afflictions having ceased, there is liberation;
   karma and afflictions arise from conceptualizations;
   these in turn arise from elaboration;
   and elaboration ceases through emptiness.

Here he gives a subtler account of the causal dynamic of causality. Birth in cyclic existence arises through the power of karma. Karma arises from afflictions (*klesha*). Afflictions arise from false projections onto objects. The term *conceptualizations* (*vikalpa*) in the verse above refers to false projections. These false projections, in turn, arise from conceptual elaborations (*prapañcha*), in particular those grasping at the intrinsic existence of objects. When the conceptual elaboration of grasping at intrinsic existence ceases through insight into emptiness, the whole nexus is destroyed. Through this, the sequence for how cyclic existence comes into being and the process for reversing it are made very clear.

We can see that here in this chapter of his work, Nagarjuna explains how what is called *cessation*—the third noble truth—is attainable. As explained before, the creation of new karma is brought to an end through directly seeing the truth, and that stage is called the *path of seeing*. At that stage, various "objects of relinquishment" are eliminated or "ceased"—such as the belief in true existence—and this is the first stage of true cessation. Later, when we have eliminated the afflictions entirely and have become an arhat, we will have then attained the final cessation.

PRESENTING THE FOURTH NOBLE TRUTH

Up to this point, we have examined the first three of the four noble truths—the suffering of samsara, the way it is perpetuated by the twelve links, and the truth of cessation. To present the fourth noble truth, the truth of the path, we can ask, "How do we meditate on the absence of conceptual elaborations that is seen by the noble ones in their direct perception of emptiness?" The rest of the eighteenth chapter of Nagarjuna's text as well as the twenty-fourth chapter present the way of this practice of the path.

Generally when we encounter terms like *conceptual elaboration*, we need to bear in mind that they mean different things in different contexts. *Conceptual elaboration*, for example, can refer to grasping at inherent existence, but it can also refer to the conceptually constructed object of such grasping. Such conceptualized, reified objects do not exist even on the conventional level, and it is these conceptual elaborations that are the object of negation in emptiness meditation. *Elaboration* can also refer to the conception of things that are empty; emptiness, as we will discuss later, is only coherent in relation to empty things, and the basis upon which emptiness is determined must itself exist. *Elaboration* can also refer simply to existence. Finally, we find the term *elaboration* in the context of what are called the *elaborations of the eight extremes:* arising and disintegration, annihilation and permanence, going and coming, and identity and difference. So the term *elaboration* can mean many things.

In the context here, *conceptual elaboration* refers to the mind that grasps at the inherent existence of phenomena.[25] When Nagarjuna writes here that this conceptual elaboration "ceases through emptiness," he means that the wisdom that realizes emptiness—and not emptiness itself—counters directly the mode of apprehension of grasping. Ignorance *grasps at* the inherent existence of all phenomena, whereas the wisdom realizing emptiness *negates* the inherent existence of phenomena. Both focus on the same object, but they relate to it in a dramatically opposed manner. Thus, it is by the realization of emptiness that grasping is eliminated.

I received the oral explanatory reading transmission of all six of Nagarjuna's analytic works from Serkong Rinpoché, and I received transmission of five of these from Khunu Rinpoché.[26] Khunu Rinpoché, who read Sanskrit well, explained to me that on the basis of the Sanskrit, the last line, "Conceptual elaborations cease through emptiness," can be read in more than one way. When the text translated as "cease through emptiness" is read in the instrumental case, then we understand it to mean that by means of realizing emptiness, conceptual elaborations come to an end, as I described above. But it can also be read in a locative sense, in which case it says that conceptual elaborations cease *within* emptiness. In other words, since self-grasping ignorance is a mental factor that, along with misconceiving phenomena in general, also misconceives the nature of the mind itself (which is by nature luminous and clear light, devoid of intrinsic existence), then when you realize emptiness, you gain insight into the true nature of the mind. When that happens, the grasping at the inherent existence of the mind that falsely conceives the nature of mind will come to an end. In this interpretation, it is within the mind's own emptiness that conceptual elaborations are pacified. Thus the last line can be read in either locative or instrumental case.

NEITHER SELF NOR SELFLESSNESS

Nagarjuna goes on:

> 6. That there is self has been stated,
>   and that there is no self has also been presented.
>   The buddhas have taught
>   that neither self nor no-self exists.

There are two different ways to read this stanza as well. In the first reading, the first line, "That there is self has been stated," refers to the non-Buddhist schools that assert a self that is some kind of independent, unitary, unchanging reality. An example is the eternal *atman,* or self, propounded by the non-Buddhist classical Indian schools, such as Samkhya. Chandrakirti defines this notion of self in *Entering the Middle Way (Madhyamakavatara)*:

That which is the partaker, an eternal entity, non-agent,

Without qualities and inactive—such a self the *tirthikas*

postulate.[27]

The second line of Nagarjuna's text refers to another ancient, non-Buddhist Indian school, the Charvaka. The Charvakas were materialists, many of whom rejected the idea of rebirth and argued that the self is only the bodily existence, such that when the body ceases, the person ends as well. Hence the second line refers to the materialistic view that rejects the existence of a self beyond bodily existence. In the first reading, the final two lines are taken to represent the Buddha's own position as contrary to the first two views: the Buddha accepts neither the notion of an eternal unchanging self nor the equation of the self with the body. The first view reifies an eternal self, while the second view reduces the self to the body of this life alone, and both of these classical Indian views are unacceptable for Nagarjuna.

In the alternate reading, the same stanza can be read so that all four lines apply to the Buddhist view. In this interpretation, we read the first line, "That there is self has been stated," to mean that the Buddha, given the diversity of mental dispositions, philosophical tendencies, and natural inclinations among his followers, made statements in some sutras suggesting there is such a thing as a self that is independent of the aggregates. For example, in one sutra Buddha states that the five aggregates are the burden and self is the carrier of that burden, which suggests a belief in some kind of autonomous self.

In this reading, the second line, "That there is no self has also been presented," shows that Buddha has also taught different levels of meaning of the no-self doctrine. These different approaches include a gross selflessness that sees no-self as rejection of self as composed of parts, which is a view of the lower Buddhist schools. The Buddha also taught no-self as the absence of a subject-object duality, which is the view of the Mind Only school. The Mind Only school teaches a doctrine of three natures, where the *perfected nature*—which is the *dependent nature* devoid of the *imputed nature*—is understood to be truly existent. In this approach, one aspect of reality is said to be devoid of self while another aspect is said to possess selfhood. Madhyamikas reject such selective application of the no-self doctrine.

Here then the last two lines are understood as the Buddha's final standpoint on the question of self and no-self: "The buddhas have taught/ that neither self nor no-self exists." Buddha not only rejected the intrinsic existence of the person, therefore teaching no-self, but he also rejected even any intrinsic, absolute existence of selflessness itself. This is the profound view of the emptiness of every single phenomenon, including even emptiness.

The theme of ensuring that we do not end up reifying emptiness comes up repeatedly in Nagarjuna's writings. Elsewhere in his text, Nagarjuna says that if even the slightest phenomenon were not devoid of inherent existence, then emptiness itself would be intrinsically real.[28] If emptiness itself were intrinsically real or absolute, then intrinsic existence could never be negated. Nagarjuna then refers to the view of grasping at the intrinsic reality of emptiness as an irreparable view that cannot be repaired or corrected.[29] Nagarjuna now explains what he means by emptiness.

A SIMPLE NEGATION

Nagarjuna goes on:

> 7. What language expresses is undone
>   because the object of mind is undone.
>   Unborn and unceased, like nirvana,
>   this is the suchness of things.

This is reminiscent of a stanza from Nagarjuna's *Sixty Verses of Reasoning* (*Yuktishashtika*), where he writes:

> Having found a locus, one is caught
> by the twisting snake of afflictions.
> Those whose minds have no locus
> are not caught by this [snake].[30]

Emptiness must be understood as a categorical negation of intrinsic existence. As long as some objectifiable basis remains, then clinging to true existence will continue to arise. When the stanza says that "What language expresses is undone," it means that emptiness—in a way that cannot be reflected in language—is utterly free of the eight extremes—arising and disintegration, annihilation and permanence, and so on. Emptiness is not like other phenomena that we can perceive; we understand and conceptualize it only by means of negation.

In their taxonomy of reality, Buddhists tend to divide phenomena into those that can be conceptualized in positive terms and those that can be conceptualized only through negation. The distinction is drawn on the basis of how we perceive or conceptualize them. Within the class of negatively characterized phenomena we find two principal forms of negation. One is *implicative negation,* which is a negation that implies the existence of something else in its place. An example would be the negation in the statement, "That mother has no son," which implies the existence of a daughter. The other type of negation is *nonimplicative negation,* which is a simple negation that implies nothing else, such as the negative statement "The Buddhist monks do not drink alcohol."

In ordinary language, we make use of these concepts. For example, when we speak of the absence of something, we might say "It is not there, but...": We are negating something, but we have left some room for further expectation. On the other hand, if we say "No, it's not there," that's a simple, categorical negation that does not suggest there is anything left to hold on to.

Emptiness is a nonimplicative negation. It is a simple, decisive negation that leaves nothing behind to grasp. The idea that emptiness must be understood as nonimplicative negation is a crucial point, emphasized repeatedly in the writings of the great Indian Madhyamaka masters like Nagarjuna and his commentators Bhavaviveka, Buddhapalita, and Chandrakirti. Bhavaviveka raised objections to Buddhapalita's interpretation of the first stanza of the first chapter in Nagarjuna's *Fundamental Stanzas on the Middle Way:*

> Neither from itself nor from another,
> nor from both, nor from no cause,
> does anything whatever
> ever arise at all anywhere.[31]

In this verse, Nagarjuna is critiquing the essentialist understanding of how things come into being. He subjects the notion of arising in terms of whether they arise from themselves, from something other than themselves, from both themselves and something else, or from neither. Nagarjuna negates all four of these alternatives, which he understands as exhaustive if the notion of arising in an essential sense were tenable. His negation of the four modes of origination is the foundation that the rest of his treatise is built upon.

In his commentary on this passage, Bhavaviveka (ca. 500–570) criticized Buddhapalita (ca. 470–530) for the way he argued against "arising from itself." Buddhapalita reasoned that if things arose from themselves, then "the arising of things would be pointless" and "things would arise *ad infinitum*." Bhavaviveka said this was unacceptable reasoning for a Madhyamika for, when the arguments are reversed, it implies that "arising has a point" and "arising is finite." In other words, it implies the existence of some kind of arising, violating a central tenet of the Madhyamaka school, which is that all theses presented in the course of analyzing emptiness must be nonimplicative negations. Emptiness is defined as the absence of all conceptual elaborations, and thus the total, categorical negation must not leave any conceivable thing remaining.

Once you understand emptiness as a nonimplicative negation and cultivate your understanding of it, your realization of emptiness will eventually become so profound that language and concepts cannot encompass it. That's why in verse 7 here, Nagarjuna wrote, "What language expresses is undone," and so on.

In the next verse he writes:

8. Everything is real and not real,
    both real and not real,
    neither real nor not real—
    this is the Buddha's teaching.

This echoes the point, raised in stanza 6, that when the Buddha taught the profound truth of the Dharma he did so by adapting his teaching to the mental capabilities of his disciples. For beginners he taught as if things existed just as they appear to the mind. Then he taught that all things are transient, in that they are subject to disintegration on a moment-by-moment basis. Finally, he taught that there is a discrepancy between the way things appear to us and the way they really are. The Buddha, says Nagarjuna, led trainees through these progressively more subtle levels of understanding.

COUNTERING MISUNDERSTANDING

From stanza 9 on, Nagarjuna provides ways to counter misunderstanding of suchness, or ultimate truth.

9. Not knowable from another, tranquil,
    not fabricated by mental elaboration,
    devoid of conceptualization, and not differentiated—
    that is the character of suchness.

This stanza presents what are known as the five main characteristics of ultimate truth. Basically, the stanza is stating that suchness lies beyond the purview of language and thought. Unlike everyday objects—where we can distinguish, say, between a thing and its properties—the emptiness that is mere negation of intrinsic existence is free of any such differentiations. It exists in the manner of a single taste. This does not mean that the suchness of all phenomena exists as one. Although each and every individual phenomenon has suchness, that just means all phenomena share the nature of being empty of intrinsic existence. That is the meaning of this stanza.

In the next stanza, we read:

10. Whatever comes into being in dependence on another
    is not identical with that thing.
    Since it is not different from that thing either,
    it is neither nonexistent nor permanent.

This stanza refers to the principle of dependent origination that we already discussed. On one level, the *dependence* in dependent origination refers to the dependence of effects upon their causes. Causality has two elements: a cause and an effect, and Nagarjuna is analyzing how these two are related to each other. What, for instance, is the relationship between a seed and a sprout? Nagarjuna is stating is that an effect cannot be identical with its cause, for were that so, then the notion of causation would become absurd. Neither could the effect be intrinsically independent from the cause, for were that so, we could not account for the obvious relationship between cause and effect—between a seed and its sprout.

Since the cause and effect are not the same, when the effect comes into being, the cause ceases to exist; the sprout and the seed it comes from do not exist simultaneously. Therefore neither cause nor effect is permanent. Yet, neither is the cause totally annihilated when the effect comes into being, and therefore it's not nonexistent.

Thus Nagarjuna concludes by stating, "As such, it is neither non-existent nor permanent."

Then we read in the next stanza:

> 11. By the buddhas, saviors of the world,
>   this immortal truth has been taught:
>   not one, not differentiated,
>   not nonexistent, and not permanent.

This stanza cautions us to be totally free of all conceptual elaborations as well as all extremes.

Up to this point, especially in stanza 5, Nagarjuna has been underscoring one of his key points, which is the necessity of cultivating the knowledge of emptiness for gaining liberation from cyclic existence. This is broadly consonant with his approach in *Sixty Verses of Reasoning*, where Nagarjuna says that realizing gross selflessness alone is not adequate; we also must realize the selflessness of phenomena. In the next stanza he extends the same argument to the *pratyekabuddhas*, the so-called self-enlightened ones.

> 12. When the fully awakened ones do not appear
>   and even the *shravakas* have disappeared,
>   the wisdom of the self-enlightened ones
>   will arise completely without reliance on others.

Just as the disciples—the *shravakas*—need the full wisdom of emptiness to gain freedom from samsara, so too do the self-enlightened ones, the *pratyekabuddhas*. There is no liberation except through the full realization of emptiness. For the bodhisattvas of the Mahayana path, the wisdom of emptiness is also the core practice, the life of the path, although that alone is not sufficient. For in the Mahayana path, the attainment of full enlightenment is said to come from the union of the *wisdom* of realizing emptiness and the *method* aspect of collecting merit and generating bodhichitta, the altruistic awakening mind. That is why emptiness in the Mahayana context is sometimes referred to as *emptiness endowed with all the enlightened qualities.*

This understanding is shared by tantra. Nagarjuna's text explains the teachings from the perspective of the Sutra or Perfection Vehicle. However, since this is an introduction to Buddhism as it flourished in Tibet, where the Vajrayana teachings were also taught, I will also address the Vajrayana perspective, the view of Buddhist tantra. According to highest yoga tantra, it is not sufficient to ascertain the emptiness that is free of conceptual elaborations such as the eight extremes. Our realization must be cultivated at the subtlest level of consciousness—at the level of the innate mind. Here *innate mind* refers to the extremely subtle consciousness that continues as a continuum from life to life. At the level of the innate mind, our awareness is totally free from all conceptual elaboration and sensory input. When the wisdom of emptiness is cultivated at this level, the practitioner progresses along the path at a rapid pace.

In his *Praise to the Ultimate Expanse,* Nagarjuna begins by saying "I pay homage to the ultimate expanse (*dharmadhatu*)." This ultimate expanse can be understood in terms of "subjective wisdom," and its full meaning as such is found in such highest yoga tantras as the *Guhyasamaja Tantra.* Subjective wisdom is there understood to mean that only when the extremely subtle consciousness—the innate mind—cognizes emptiness can the mental elaborations be calmed.

Jamyang Shepa (1648–1721), near the end of his major work on the philosophical tenets where he identifies the unique features of Vajrayana teachings, explains that although the sutra-level teachings explain the supreme object (emptiness), the supreme subject—the wisdom of the innate mind—remains hidden and must be found instead in the Vajrayana. Similarly, he states that while the sutras describe the principal antidotes on the path, the highest antidote is hidden.[32] This is the antidote for removing the subtle obstructions to knowledge that prevent full enlightenment. His point is that to attain full enlightenment, it is not enough to cultivate the wisdom of emptiness and practice the six perfections at the level of the ordinary, gross mind. The special insight into emptiness must be cultivated at the subtlest level of consciousness, the innate mind, as well. The approaches of Great Perfection (*Dzokchen*), Great Seal (*Mahamudra*), and spontaneous wisdom of the union of bliss and emptiness all engage on that level.

AFFLICTIONS AND THEIR IMPRINTS

There are two important points about the afflictions to bear in mind. First is that, in general, all the mental afflictions—afflicted thoughts and emotions—are distorted; they do not reflect the way things really are. Given their distorted nature, powerful antidotes exist to help eradicate them. Second, the essential nature of mind is luminous—clear light. When we combine these two premises—the polluted nature of the afflictions and the clear-light nature of the mind—then we can begin to envision the possibility of eradicating these pollutants from our minds. Liberation from cyclic existence becomes conceivable.

We need to apply that same reasoning to our *propensity* for these afflictions, the imprints left on our mindstream by these afflictions. These imprints are what are specifically meant by the *subtle obscurations*, or the *obstructions to knowledge*. Just as the afflictions are removable, their propensities are also removable; they do not reflect the essential nature of the mind. Knowing this allows us to envision not only liberation from samsara, but also the possibility of full enlightenment, or buddhahood—which is total freedom from not just afflictions but also their imprints.

The afflictions can be eradicated by cultivating deep insight into emptiness, which directly opposes the mode of apprehension of ignorance and grasping. But as far as their imprints are concerned, that approach alone is not adequate. Among the subtle obscurations, there is a defilement that obstructs us from having a simultaneous experience of the two truths—conventional truth and ultimate truth. We tend to misperceive the two truths as having distinct natures. Until that defilement is overcome, all our realization of emptiness, even the direct realization of emptiness, will only alternate with what are called *subsequent realizations*—positive realizations that pertain to the conventional truth, such as karmic causation and the four noble truths. When subsequent realization occurs, the meditative equipoise on emptiness ceases, and vice versa.

The only way to experience deep meditative equipoise and subsequent realization simultaneously, and to overcome this perception that the two truths are essentially different, is by bringing about that realization of emptiness at the subtlemost level of consciousness. What is required is the merging of the ultimate meaning, which is emptiness, and the ultimate mind, which is the innate mind of clear light. When this occurs, then appearances and emptiness no longer appear separately, and the subtle defilements are overcome.

4. Establishing Conventional Truth

In Nagarjuna's treatise, the twenty-fourth chapter, "Examination of the Four Noble Truths," is uniquely important. In the chapters that precede it, Nagarjuna presented a series of related arguments, all intended to demolish grasping at any form of intrinsic existence whatsoever. On the level of everyday perception, phenomena are manifold, but on the ultimate level, all of them are revealed to be devoid of intrinsic existence. This argument regarding the emptiness of intrinsic existence of all phenomena can raise all sorts of doubts in the mind. Chapter 24 addresses these doubts directly.

PRESENTING THE OBJECTIONS

Some individuals, lacking an affinity for the teachings of emptiness, understand the emptiness of inherent existence to really imply nothingness. Even the great Buddhist thinker Asanga (ca. fourth century) criticized Madhyamaka philosophers as nihilistic in one of his texts. He says in his *Compendium of the Great Vehicle* (*Mahayanasamgraha*) that some who claimed to be Mahayanists failed to understand the Perfection of Wisdom sutras and denigrated reality by asserting that all phenomena are devoid of inherent existence. Of course, renowned for having attained the third bodhisattva ground, Asanga's own understanding of emptiness was therefore that of the Madhyamaka. In his historical role as founder of the Mind Only school, however, he criticized the Madhyamaka followers as falling into nihilism.

There are others who, while ostensibly admiring the teachings of emptiness and Madhyamaka philosophy, still mistakenly understand the emptiness teachings in a nihilistic fashion. Such people may have a tendency to say things like, "Oh nothing really matters—everything is empty after all." When you say things like that, you risk denigrating the validity of the conventional world and the law of cause and effect.

Given the danger of such misunderstanding, Nagarjuna deliberately raises the potential objections to his teaching on emptiness and responds to them one by one. The primary objection, in essence, goes something like this: "In the preceding chapters you negated the intrinsic existence of all phenomena from the perspectives of their causation, their production of effects, their own nature, their defining characteristics, and so on. If you are correct in stating that nothing exists in terms of its nature and causes, inherently, then in the final analysis nothing exists at all, and therefore there is no fruit of the path. The teaching on emptiness is mere nihilism." This is the main objection Nagarjuna echoes and responds to in this chapter. For this reason, chapter 24 may be the most important chapter of Nagarjuna's *Fundamental Wisdom of the Middle Way.*

In the first six stanzas Nagarjuna raises the primary objections against the teaching of emptiness:

> 1. If all of this is empty,
>   neither arising nor disintegrating,
>   then for you, it follows that
>   the four noble truths do not exist.

2. If the four noble truths do not exist,
    then knowledge, abandonment,
    cultivation, and actualization
    are [all] untenable.

3. If these things do not exist,
    the four fruits also do not exist.
    Without the fruits, there is no attainer of the fruits,
    nor are there those who enter [the paths].

4. If these eight kinds of person do not exist,[33]
    the spiritual community would not exist;
    and since the noble truths do not exist,
    the sublime Dharma would also not exist.

5. If Dharma and spiritual community do not exist,
    how can there be a Buddha?
    Therefore if you speak of emptiness,
    this undermines the Three Jewels.

6. It undermines everything—
    the existence of fruits,
    [the distinction between] immoral and moral actions—
    [in brief,] all conventions of the world.

These verses object that if nothing possesses intrinsic existence, then nothing in fact exists. If the emptiness of inherent existence did in fact mean nothingness or nonexistence, then indeed nothing whatsoever would be tenable and no coherent presentation of any system could be maintained.

Nagarjuna responds to the foregoing verses by saying:

7.   You who speak in these terms
       have failed to understand the purpose of emptiness,
       emptiness itself, and the meaning of emptiness.
       You are therefore harmed by it.

All of these objections to emptiness arise when you fail to fully understand emptiness—its purpose, its nature, and its meaning.

The purpose of emptiness is as was presented earlier in verse 5 of chapter 18, where Nagarjuna says that "Karma and afflictions arise from conceptualizations;/ these in turn arise from elaboration;" and so on. Here *elaboration* is identified as fundamental ignorance, the first link in the chain of dependent origination. Since ignorance or elaboration lies at the root of our samsaric state, only by meditating on the emptiness that is free of elaborations can we find our way to liberation.

When Nagarjuna says, in the first verse of chapter 26, "Obscured by ignorance and for the sake of rebirth," *ignorance* for him is not a passive unknowing. Ignorance is a *mis*knowing, an actively afflicted intelligence. Such mental states, while false, bring with them a degree of certainty that seems to arise from the depth of our thinking. To counter them, therefore, we must apply antidotes that also engender a powerful certitude; there is other means to counter them effectively. Insight into emptiness directly opposes that grasping mind and thus brings about freedom.

Therefore the true purpose of realizing emptiness is not simply to enhance our knowledge but to free us from cyclic existence. No one desires suffering, and so we must eliminate its causes. We cannot eliminate suffering through prayer or even through ending our own lives. To dispel the root cause of suffering, the delusion grasping at the true existence of things, we need to gain insight into emptiness. Apart from insight into emptiness, there's really no other alternative.

When we look at our afflicted thoughts and emotions, we see, on the one hand, emotions such as attachment, aversion, and pride. These are impulsive and instinctual. While there may be some element of analysis present, on the whole they arise spontaneously, without the need for any reasoning process. On the other hand, we find other afflictions referred to in the texts as "afflicted intelligence," which includes the grasping at intrinsic existence, as mentioned above. These are not instinctive emotions but rather thoughts that tend to reinforce our false views.

Thus afflictions are divided into the impulsive, instinctual affective states, like attachment, and the more cognitive delusions, such as ignorance. Each requires different antidotes. For example, an antidote to attachment might include meditations on the impurity of a particular object; to counter strong hatred, we might cultivate loving-kindness. Antidotes like this, however, cannot totally eradicate the afflictions; they can only lessen them. Furthermore, as Chandrakirti points out in his commentary on Nagarjuna's stanzas, meditating on love to counter hatred can inadvertently induce attachment to the object, since you are enhancing your sense of connection, empathy, and intimacy toward it. Similarly, when you counter attachment by reflecting upon faults in the chosen object, you might inadvertently develop a form of aversion to that object. For example, meditating on the impurity of the human body is an antidote to lust, but pursuing this meditation could increase your aversion to other beings. The antidote to ignorance—the realization of emptiness—has no such side effect. The wisdom of emptiness not only counters grasping at inherent existence, it can also counter and eradicate all the other afflictions as well. This is because the delusion of intrinsic existence lies at the root of all the afflictions.

Prasangika Madhyamikas understand afflictions more broadly than do Buddhists in general. That afflictions such as attachment and aversion have gross and subtle levels is an important insight Tsongkhapa arrived at through a long process of analysis. Tsongkhapa distinguishes between the afflictions presented in the Abhidharma system on the one hand, which are accepted by all Buddhist schools, and more subtle level of afflictions that only the Prasangika Madhyamaka system identifies on the other.[34] Broadly speaking, I understand the distinction as follows.

The generally accepted understanding of afflictions is that they possess distinct objects of focus and disturb the mind in distinct ways. Attachment, for instance, exaggerates the attractive qualities of a desired object, while aversion exaggerates negative qualities. In the Prasangika system, however, all afflictions involve, in their mode of apprehension, an element of grasping at intrinsic existence. Whether attachment, aversion, pride, or some other mental state, what makes them afflictions is not their distinct character but this common denominator of grasping at self-existence when apprehending its object.

Since the variety of mental states that grasp their objects to be intrinsically existent is not limited to the afflictions as enumerated in the Abhidharma texts, the Prasangika Madhyamaka definition of an affliction is much broader than the general definition.

Prasangikas, therefore, identify as afflictions many mental states that other Buddhist schools, from Svatantrika Madhyamaka on down, do not. Does this mean that for Prasangikas all afflictions are simply forms of ignorance, the delusion of grasping at true existence? Tsongkhapa distinguishes between the delusion of grasping at true existence itself on the one hand and mental states, such as attachment and aversion, that merely possess an element of grasping at true existence on the other. The former grasps at true existence not through the power of some accompanying factor but through its own power. Other afflicted mental states, in contrast, grasp at true existence not due to their own power but through the power of an accompanying factor. They involve grasping at true existence but are defined primarily by other characteristics.

In brief, the gross level of afflictions arises from having delusion grasping at true existence as the cause, while the subtle level of afflictions arises when a mental state is conjoined with delusion grasping at true existence. The purpose of emptiness is to generate the antidote to the delusion grasping at true existence of things. Since all afflictions, both gross and subtle, are driven by this delusion, the antidote to all the afflictions is to directly contradict the perspective of this grasping.

Having looked at the purpose of emptiness, we now turn to examining its nature. Fundamental to the misunderstanding of emptiness as nothingness is the failure to recognize that language and concepts alone cannot adequately encompass emptiness. If we never leave the domain of concepts, then it is natural to think of emptiness as one concept among many. Confined to this sphere, it is easy to go from the correct view that "everything is empty" to the erroneous view that "nothing exists." The error comes from taking an object's lack of intrinsic existence—its ultimate nature—and making that ultimate nature an object in its own right. If the ultimate nature of everything is an absence, the reasoning goes, then it must be that nothing exists. But emptiness is separate from the object that is empty only on a conceptual level and not in actuality. For this reason, emptiness is something the true nature of which can only be experienced personally and for oneself. It cannot be fully conveyed to another person by means of language and concepts.

When we speak of emptiness, therefore, do not think of it as some kind of absolute entity that exists out there on its own. When we speak of it, we are speaking of the ultimate mode of being, the ultimate way a phenomenon exists. This ultimate mode of being is only coherent in relation to individual phenomena. It is a mistake to think of emptiness as if it were an absolute, independent of the various phenomena that it characterizes. It is understanding emptiness in this way that leads to the mistake of misunderstanding it as nothingness.

Having discussed the purpose of emptiness and its nature, the third point raised by Nagarjuna is that it is due to a misunderstanding of the *meaning* of emptiness that such objections are raised. To explain the correct meaning of emptiness, he alludes to a passage from the sutra entitled *Questions of the Naga King Anavatapta,* in which the Buddha explains that "That which has arisen in dependence on others is unborn."[35] He is stating that things and events cannot possess intrinsic origination because, as phenomena, they originate in dependence on other factors. They are "unborn" in the sense that they do not arise autonomously. His point is that emptiness must be understood in terms of dependent origination. Something with an inherent nature is by definition self-enclosed or independent and cannot therefore be subject to dependence. Intrinsic existence and dependent nature are mutually exclusive. Therefore anything that comes into being in dependence on other factors must be devoid of inherent existence.

Madhyamaka texts, in their focus on the negation of inherent existence, make use of many types of arguments. The argument for the absence of identity and difference, for example, undercuts belief in intrinsic existence by analyzing whether two related phenomena are the same or not; the "diamond slivers" argument negates the four possibilities of origination; and there are others as well. However, all of these, in the final analysis, must converge on the argument of dependent origination, because in the final analysis, the ultimate proof of emptiness is dependent origination.

The meaning of emptiness is dependent origination.

DEPENDENT DESIGNATION

I explained above how the meaning of dependent origination can be understood as the dependence of effects on their causes: If things existed intrinsically, then causes and their effects would exist in isolation from each other, bringing the absurd conclusion that effects would not require causes to arise. However, from Nagarjuna's point of view, the meaning of dependent origination must be taken further and understood not only as causal dependence but also as *dependent designation*—the idea that the identity of a thing can only be conceived in dependence on other factors and not in and of itself.

For example, all phenomena that we conceive, both conditioned and unconditioned, can be understood in relation to the concept of the whole and its parts—the constituted and its constituent elements. Anything that is constituted has constituent elements, and there is a mutual dependence between the parts and the whole. Only in relation to such dependence can we conceive the identities of all phenomena. This is one kind of dependent designation.

However, Nagarjuna takes it to an even deeper level of subtlety. Not only are phenomena dependent on their component parts, but if we probe among the parts, we can find nothing that we can point to and say, "here is the real thing, the defining characteristic." Things come to be known as particular things only on the basis of their *designative bases*. Dependent designation, then, means that things exist by way of being labeled upon a suitable basis or through worldly convention. In other words, they are dependent on their designation by the mind conceiving them, because all phenomena in the final analysis are conceptual labels applied on aggregations of certain bases. Their identity cannot be separated from the conceptual mind that labels them.

Some Madhyamaka masters, while agreeing that phenomena exist by virtue of being designated in accordance with the way they appear to the mind, nonetheless accept the notion of a self-defining character on the conventional level. They largely accept dependent designation, but if we analyze their standpoint carefully, we find a residual assumption of something that *can* be perceived by the mind, some shred of objective existence. Madhyamaka philosophy masters who reject the notion of a self-defining characteristic even on the conventional level raise this objection: "If this were true, we could simply point to the thing itself and say, 'this is it.' This we cannot do. Things may appear to possess objective reality, but this is a mere projection; such a reality cannot be found by analysis and therefore has no basis, even conventionally." Based on such divergence of standpoints, there arose differences in opinion, including whether true existence—which is the object of negation—appears to sensory perceptions, or whether there can be a mutually verified common subject.

In any case, according to Nagarjuna, when we search for an essence, nothing on the part of the object can withstand critical analysis to be identified as the thing itself. Anything that we search for will reveal its nature to be thoroughly dependent. Nothing stands apart as an absolute, unique, independent entity. There are only two ways in which we can understand the existence, or ontological status, of things: either as possessing some kind of intrinsic, independent, objective reality or as dependent designations. There is no other choice. Since an objective existence of things turns out to be untenable, the only choice left is nominal existence or reality. It is not merely that things cannot be found when sought critically; things exist in terms of dependent designation. And even this existence on the basis of designation can only be posited within a relative framework. No things possess independent status.

If our understanding of emptiness is that of dependent origination, then the term itself negates any mistaken view of emptiness as nothingness. Thus master Tsongkhapa writes in his *Praise to Dependent Origination:*

"It is through the reasoning of dependent origination
that one does not lean toward an extreme."
That you've declared this excellently is the reason,
O Savior, that you are an unexcelled speaker.[36]

As Tsongkhapa points out here, just using the term *dependent orig-ination* has the power to dispel the extremes of both absolutism and nihilism. This is because the term *dependent* dispels absolutism by revealing the dependent nature of all things, while the term *origina-tion* dispels the extreme of nihilism because it doesn't refer to noth-ing but rather to something that comes into being. Only when you fail to understand emptiness in terms of dependent origination do all these questions about whether emptiness implies nihilism arise. People who object that emptiness is a form of nihilism, Nagarjuna states in stanza 7, have failed to appreciate the purpose of emptiness, have not properly grasped the nature of emptiness, and have failed to understand its meaning.

DISTINGUISHING PROPERLY

Then the question arises that if nothing really possesses inherent existence, still, our day-to-day experiences suggest to us that things possess some kind of objective reality. We touch, feel, and see things. When we contact certain things, we feel pain. Other things bring us pleasurable sensations. It is natural to relate to the world and its contents as if they had some kind of objective, intrinsic nature. For the realists, this is the highest proof that things must possess intrinsic reality: the tangibility of objects, the vividness of the experience.

In response to this question, Nagarjuna answered that yes, on the level of appearance we do experience diverse phenomena and do tend to perceive things and events as if they possessed intrinsic reality. He is not denying the robust reality of our conventional experiences. But their underlying reality is something else. There is a gap between our perceptions and reality. This is where Nagarjuna presents the two truths, conventional and ultimate.

8. The Buddha's teaching of the Dharma
    is based entirely on the two truths—
    the truth of worldly convention
    and the ultimate truth.

9. Those who do not understand
    the distinction between the two truths
    do not understand
    the Buddha's profound teaching.

10. Without a basis in the conventional truth
    the truth of the ultimate cannot be taught;
    without understanding the ultimate truth,
    nirvana will not be attained.

Within the world of conventional truth—the world of conceptual constructs—a distinction is made between real and unreal conventions. Although nothing exists that is not designated by the mind, this does not entail that whatever the mind posits can be said to exist. In other words, just because we can conjure something up with our minds does not make it real. This is an extremely important point. We need to distinguish between what is real and what is not on the conventional level.

How do we make such a determination? If something we know conventionally is invalidated or contradicted by another valid experience—whether our own or another's—then it is unreal. Numerous perceptions that are effected by sensory distortions—such as the perception of falling hairs caused by an ophthalmic disorder—do not exist even on the conventional level. Similarly, we may adopt concepts through either philosophical speculation or other absolutist ways of thinking that can be invalidated by other conventional knowledge. Postulations adopted through an incomplete investigation of the ontological status of things can be invalidated through ultimate analysis.

In summary, then, for something to be posited as conventionally existent, it must meet the following three criteria:

1. It must be familiar to the world's convention;
2. It must not be invalidated by other conventionally valid knowledge; and
3. It must also not be invalidated by ultimate analysis.

This may be a little confusing, but we may understand it better if we relate it to our personal experience. For example, sometimes people ask us about something we have seen. We can say, "Yes, that's the truth. I have seen it. Not only did I see it, I carefully examined it and made sure that what I thought I saw was accurate." When we see something, carefully examine it, and believe it to be true, and then a second person comes along and verifies it, then that can be said to be real in the conventional sense.

On the other hand, we might see something that upon closer examination turns out to be other than what we thought it was. Or we may insist something is so even though we haven't examined it carefully, and then a second person comes along and fails to verify it. This is an indication that our earlier perception was not true and that what we saw was unreal. Furthermore, some points made by philosophers may hold up to valid convention but be invalidated by an investigation of the ultimate truth of things. Thus, those things that are said to be real from the perspective of worldly convention are those that cannot be invalidated by our own subsequent examination, by the correct knowledge of a second person, or by an ultimate analysis.

> 11. By viewing emptiness wrongly,
>   a person of little intelligence is destroyed,
>   like a snake incorrectly seized
>   or a spell incorrectly cast.

> 12. Thus knowing that it is difficult
>   to penetrate the depth of this teaching,
>   the Buddha's thought turned away
>   from teaching this [profound] Dharma.

> 13. You've raised fallacious objections.
>   Since they are not relevant to emptiness,
>   your [objections] from abandonment
>   of emptiness do not apply to me.

Then as a grand summary, Nagarjuna writes:

> 14. For whom emptiness is tenable
>   for him everything becomes tenable;
>   for whom emptiness is untenable
>   for him everything becomes untenable.

Based on this reasoning he writes, referring to objections of the realists:

> 15. When you throw upon us
>   all of your own faults,
>   you are like a man riding his horse
>   who has forgotten where his horse is!

In the following stanzas, he turns all the objections raised against the Madhyamaka school back onto the Buddhist realists' own position:

> 16. If you view the existence of things
>   in terms of intrinsic nature,
>   you are then viewing things
>   as having no causes and conditions.

> 17. Effects and their causes;
>   agent, action, and object of action;
>   arising and disintegration;
>   you undermine all these as well.

Again the point is that inherent existence and causal dependence are mutually exclusive. If something has an inherent nature, it is complete in itself, without relying on any causal process. A causal process implies a susceptibility to being effected, but if a thing is fully self-enclosed and complete in itself, it can't interact with other phenomena. Nagarjuna is saying, therefore, that if you insist on the intrinsic existence of things, you are thereby maintaining that things have no causes and conditions.

His point is also that all of these concepts are relative terms, and because of that, they can only be coherently understood within a relative context with a specific point of reference. For example, when we say something is harmful or beneficial, the point of reference is a sentient being to whom something is beneficial or harmful. Similarly, when we say "action," the point of reference is the agent committing the act. When we say "an agent," it is in relation to the action that is done. The conception of all such things can only occur within the relative context. If you asserted their inherent existence, you would thereby reject cause and effect and the possibility of change, and none of these terms could be coherently maintained.

In stanza 18, Nagarjuna reaffirms that the true meaning of emptiness is dependent origination:

18. Whatever is dependently originated,
     that is explained to be emptiness.
     That, being a dependent designation,
     is itself the middle way.

19. That which is not dependently originated,
     such a thing does not exist.
     Therefore, that which is not empty,
     such a thing does not exist.

Here, dependent origination is understood not in terms of causes and effects but in terms of dependent designation. From that perspective, all phenomena—both conditioned and unconditioned—are dependently originated, and all phenomena are thereby empty. Dependent origination is therefore the true middle way (*madhyamaka*) and the essential meaning of the teachings of the Buddha.

FLAWS IN THE ESSENTIALIST POSITION

From stanza 20 onward Nagarjuna refutes all the objections to the Madhyamaka view by the "essentialists"—those who believe in inherent existence—and raises objections of his own against the essentialist position. First, through to stanza 27, Nagarjuna shows that within a system that holds a belief in intrinsic existence, the teachings of the four noble truths cannot be maintained.

> 20. If all of this is not empty,
>   neither origination nor disintegration,
>   then it follows for you that
>   the four noble truths do not exist.

> 21. If things are not dependent originations,
>   how does suffering come to be?
>   Suffering has been taught to be impermanent,
>   so how can it exist from its intrinsic nature?

> 22. If things exist from their intrinsic nature,
>   what then is the origin of suffering?
>   Therefore, for he who objects to emptiness,
>   there is no origin of suffering.

> 23. If suffering existed inherently,
>   there would be no cessation.

Since intrinsic nature abides,
one undermines true cessation.

24. If the path possessed inherent existence,
cultivation would become impossible.
Since the path is indeed cultivated,
it must not have your intrinsic nature.

25. Now if suffering, its origin,
and cessation are nonexistent,
by what path can one seek
the attainment of the cessation of suffering?

26. If non-knowledge comes to be
through its intrinsic nature,
how can knowledge arise?
Does not intrinsic nature abide?

27. Similarly, just as with knowledge,
your relinquishment, actualization,
cultivation, and the four fruits—
these will become untenable.

Up to this point, Nagarjuna has been demonstrating how the four noble truths become untenable for someone who subscribes to the notion of inherent existence. He then demonstrated how, if the four noble truths become untenable, the four fruits—that is the four attainments—as well as the four persons who attain these fruits and the four persons who enter the paths leading to the four fruits would all become untenable. If this happens, the Three Jewels—the Sangha, Dharma, and the Buddha—also become untenable. Thus Nagarjuna writes:

28. For you who uphold intrinsic nature
    the fruits would already be realized
    through their intrinsic nature;
    so in what way can they be attained?

29. Without the fruits, there would be no attainer of the
        fruits;
    there would be no enterers as well.
    And if the eight kinds of person do not exist,
    there would be no spiritual community.

30. Given that the four noble truths do not exist,
    the sublime Dharma too would not exist;
    If the Dharma and spiritual community do not exist
    how can a Buddha come to be?

31. For you, it would follow that a Buddha
    would arise without dependence upon enlightenment,
    and for you, enlightenment would arise
    without dependence upon a Buddha.

32. For you, one who was unenlightened
    through his intrinsic nature,
    even by practicing the path to enlightenment,
    he could not attain enlightenment.

Nagarjuna then demonstrates how, if things possess intrinsic existence, the distinction between moral and immoral actions—that is, the distinction between beneficial and harmful actions—becomes untenable. In brief, he argues that the entire moral law of karma falls apart if things are intrinsically existent. Thus he writes:

> 33. No one could ever perform
>   moral or immoral actions;
>   if things are nonempty, what could one do?
>   In intrinsic nature there is no activity.

> 34. For you, it follows that effects would arise
>   with no [corresponding] moral or immoral actions.
>   Thus for you the effects that came into being
>   from moral and immoral actions would not exist.

> 35. If, for you, effects that come from
>   moral and immoral actions do exist,
>   why then are these effects that come from
>   moral and immoral actions not empty?

Only emptiness makes sense

Nagarjuna is now raising a broader objection to the realist position, showing how the intelligibility of experience itself is not possible in a world where things exist by virtue of an intrinsic nature.

> 36. He who rejects this emptiness
>   of dependent origination

undermines as well
all worldly conventions.

37. For if emptiness itself is rejected,
     no functions will remain;
     there would be uninitiated actions,
     and there would be agents without action.

38. If there is intrinsic existence, the whole world
     will be non-arising, non-disintegrating,
     and will last for all eternity,
     devoid of varying states.

39. If empty things do not exist,
     then attainment of what is not attained,
     termination of suffering, as well as karma
     and the elimination of afflictions would not exist.

If we espouse a belief in intrinsic existence, then nothing, no conventional knowledge, can be coherently maintained. For example, if we analyze the concepts that we use in our day-to-day experience, we will find that a lot of our experiences are based on memories of things that have already occurred. Similarly, many of the terms we use and the concepts that go with them are constructed on the basis of some anticipated future. In this way our conventional reality and the terms and language that give it definition arise conditioned by memory of the past and anticipation of the future, comprised of entities and people that exist and change over time.

Nagarjuna argues that if our understanding of the world is constructed in dependence on memories and expectations, then our reality cannot be comprised of independent, inherently existent entities. If it were, the concept of all these functions and actions we take for granted would have no real coherence. Likewise, he continues, in a self-existent world, beings would never change over time, and no spiritual attainments would be possible.

In conclusion, Nagarjuna summarizes that only those who see that the true meaning of emptiness is dependent origination will comprehend the true nature of suffering and therefore be able to maintain coherently the teachings of the four noble truths: suffering, its origin, cessation, and the path. So, summarizing all of these critical points presented above, Nagarjuna writes:

40. Whoever sees dependent origination
    sees [the truth of] suffering,
    its origin and cessation,
    and the path [to cessation].

This then is chapter 24, the chapter on the analysis of the four noble truths, from Nagarjuna's *Fundamental Wisdom of the Middle Way*, and here ends the first part of our exploration.

To explore the method for putting these teachings into practice, we will now turn our attention to another seminal text.

Part II

An Exploration of Tsongkhapa's
Three Principal Aspects of the Path

5. *Practicing the Profound*

Up to this point I have presented, based on an explanation of three crucial chapters from Nagarjuna's *Fundamental Wisdom of the Middle Way*, the basic framework of the Buddhist path. We shall now move on to the second part, which is how to bring all these understandings together within a framework for actual Dharma practice. This I will explain on the basis of Tsongkhapa's short text, *Three Principal Aspects of the Path*. The three aspects that Tsongkhapa addresses in his text are true renunciation, the altruistic awakening mind (*bodhichitta*), and the correct view of emptiness.

A FIRM FOUNDATION

To first return briefly to the prayer I wrote, *Praise to Seventeen Nalanda Masters*, we read earlier:

> By understanding the two truths, the way things exist,
> I will ascertain how, through the four truths, we enter and
>   exit samsara;
> I will make firm the faith in the Three Jewels that is born of
>   valid reason.
> May I be blessed so that the root of the liberating path is
>   firmly established within me.

If we develop a profound understanding of the meaning of Dharma based on deep reflection on the teachings on the twelve links and the view of emptiness presented in the preceding chapters, we will plant the seed of liberation within our minds. We begin of course with an intellectual understanding derived from study, but once we have some intellectual understanding of the importance of emptiness, we begin to sense the possibility of gaining freedom from cyclic existence. The possibility of nirvana or liberation and the methods to attain it become more real for us, more tangible.

With this kind of understanding, we get a deeper understanding of what is meant by Dharma. It is the true cessation of afflictions. The path leading to it is also the Dharma. Once we have a deeper understanding of the meaning of the Dharma Jewel, we will have a deeper understanding of the meaning of the Sangha, who embody the realization of Dharma at different levels of experience. And once we have that kind of understanding, we can envision a true Buddha Jewel, who represents the perfection of the realization and knowledge of Dharma. Thus we develop a deep faith in the Three Jewels grounded on a deep understanding of their nature. In this way we establish the foundation of the path to liberation.

If we have such a profound understanding of the nature of the Three Jewels, grounded on a deep understanding of the teachings of the four noble truths, and based on an understanding of emptiness, then we will have a deep recognition of the unenlightened nature of our existence. When, on this basis, we develop a deeply felt determination and a genuine aspiration to gain freedom from this ignorance, that is *true renunciation.* That is also a true aspiration for liberation.

Once we have achieved that realization of renunciation and we redirect our focus onto other sentient beings and reflect upon their suffering condition, this will lead to the realization of great compassion. As we cultivate that great compassion further, that great compassion acquires a tremendous sense of courage and responsibility. At that point, our great compassion is known as *extraordinary compassion,* or the *extraordinary altruistic resolve.* When that compassion is developed further still, it will eventually culminate in the realization of *bodhichitta,* the altruistic awakening mind, which is endowed with two aspirations—the aspiration to bring about others' welfare and the aspiration to seek buddhahood for this purpose. That is the progression by which we realize genuine bodhichitta.

A SYSTEMATIC APPROACH

You can see that the foundation of bodhichitta—and indeed of all attainments in Buddhism—is true renunciation. However, such realization of renunciation can only arise on the basis of gradual systematic training—through a series of graduated practices. In the first stage, you cultivate various methods to diminish excessive preoccupation with the concerns of this life. Once you have gained that, then you cultivate practices to overcome excessive preoccupation with the concerns of future lives. With those practices, you gradually generate a genuine aspiration to attain freedom from cyclic existence.

In the writings of the fourth-century master Asanga, different terms are used to refer to practitioners of different levels—practitioners of initial stages, intermediate stages, advanced stages, and so on. It is on the basis of Asanga's distinctions among levels of practitioners that Atisha (982–1054), in his work *Lamp for the Path to*

Enlightenment (*Bodhipathapradipa*), presents the entire elements of the Buddha's path within the framework of the practices of the three scopes—initial scope, intermediate scope, and advanced scope.

Atisha's sequential approach found its way into all four main schools of Tibetan Buddhism. In the Nyingma tradition, for example, Longchenpa (1308–64), particularly in his text *Mind at Ease*, presents a systematic sequence to the basic framework of the path in terms of what is called "turning the mind away from four false attitudes," and we find the same approach in his *Treasury of the Wish-Fulfilling Gem*.[37] In the Kagyü tradition, Gampopa's (1079–1153) *Jewel Ornament of Liberation* presents a similar gradual, systematic approach to the path, where training the mind is presented in terms of the four thoughts that turn the mind toward Dharma. We also find a similar approach in the Sakya tradition in the teachings on the path and fruition (*lamdré*), where emphasis is placed on overcoming appearances and so on in a systematic, gradual way. Sakya Pandita's (1182–1251) *Clarifying the Buddha's Intent* also adopts a similar systematic approach. Finally, the Geluk school—with its teachings on the stages of the path to enlightenment (*lamrim*)—explicitly follows Atisha's approach.

Thus we can see that, broadly speaking, the systematic approach of training the mind to first recognize the value of human existence, then to cultivate renunciation, and so on, which is present in all the four main schools of Tibetan Buddhism, is based on the sequence presented in Atisha's *Lamp for the Path to Enlightenment*.

If we look at our own experience, we can also see the value of the systematic approach to practice. For example, if we reflect carefully, we will recognize that, to develop a genuine aspiration to be free from cyclic existence, a genuine aspiration for nirvana, we have to find a way to overcome attachment to the excellences or pleasures of this unenlightened existence. As long as we do not have that genuine sense of turning away from the qualities and riches of cyclic existence, the wish for liberation will never be genuine. This suggests that we must find a way to turn our mind away from preoccupation with the fate of our status in samsara. To turn our mind away from preoccupation with the concerns of a future life, we need first of all to be able to turn our mind away from obsession with the affairs of this life. For if we are totally absorbed with the concerns of this life, the yearning for a better future in a future life won't arise in the first place.

The way we short-circuit that excessive preoccupation is by reflecting deeply upon impermanence and the transient nature of life. When we reflect on the transient nature of life, the thought to take care of our future fate becomes more important. In a similar way, excessive preoccupation with the concerns of future lives is diminished by reflecting upon karmic cause and effect, and particularly upon the defects of cyclic existence.

In terms of earlier textual sources for this systematic approach to training the mind, we can cite Aryadeva's *Four Hundred Stanzas on the Middle Way*. Aryadeva was a principal student of Nagarjuna, and his work begins with the pledge of composition before plunging into the heart of his presentation. It's significant to note that there is no customary salutation verse because he intended the work to be a supplement to Nagarjuna's *Fundamental Stanzas on the Middle Way*.

In *Four Hundred Stanzas on the Middle Way*, Aryadeva writes the following:

> First, we must cease demeritorious deeds;
> second, we must cease [grasping at] selfhood;
> and finally, we must cease [clinging to] all views.
> One who knows such a way is truly wise.[38]

This stanza presents the systematic order for the practice of training the mind.

Generally speaking, Tsongkhapa wrote three important texts on the stages of the path to enlightenment (*lamrim*): the *Great Treatise on the Stages of the Path,* the *Middle-Length Stages of the Path,* and then the shortest version, *Lines of Experience.*[39] All of these stages of the path texts, again, present a systematic order of the training of the mind. For example, they begin with the contemplation of the value and potential of human existence, which is endowed with opportunities and leisure not afforded to lower realms of existence. This is followed by the contemplation of the certainty and imminence of death—the transient nature of life—which is then followed by seeking refuge in the Three Jewels, followed by its precept, which is living life according to karmic law of cause and effect. Together these contemplations and actions present a complete set of practices for the practitioners of the initial scope of aspiration.

In a sense, in the lamrim texts, the specific set of practices corresponding to each person—whether of initial, intermediate, or great scope—can be seen as complete in themselves. So, for instance, the section on initial scope presents the entire elements of the path necessary to fulfill the spiritual aspiration of the initial scope, which is to attain favorable rebirth. Likewise, the intermediate scope, which includes the initial scope within it, contains all the practices necessary to attain its goal, which is liberation from cyclic existence.

Finally, the great-scope practices, when combined with the practices of the two preceding scopes, are sufficient to bring the practitioner to the goal of complete enlightenment.

The short text that we are dealing with here, the *Three Principal Aspects of the Path*, though belonging to the stages of the path genre, presents some of the elements of the practices in a slightly different order. For example, the meditation on karma is presented in the context of overcoming preoccupations with the concerns of future lives.

RENUNCIATION

Now we read from Tsongkhapa's text, which as is customary begins with a salutation:

Homage to the most venerable teachers!

This salutation encompasses the practice of proper reliance upon a qualified spiritual teacher, which is the foundation for all the higher qualities of not only this life but also future lives. The salutation is made to the teachers to emphasize that point.

Then, in the first stanza, we read:

1. **I will explain here to the best of my ability
    the essential points of all the scriptures of the
        Conqueror,
        the path acclaimed by all excellent bodhisattvas,
        the gateway for fortunate ones aspiring for liberation.**

In this stanza, the author pledges to compose the text. In the second stanza, he urges those with fortunate karma to listen to what he is presenting. He writes:

2. Those who are not attached to the joys of cyclic existence,
   who strive to make meaningful this life of leisure and opportunities
   and who place their trust in the path that pleases the conquerors—
   O fortunate ones, listen with an open heart.

The next three stanzas together present the first principal aspect of the path—true renunciation. The third explains the importance of cultivating true renunciation. The fourth presents the actual method for cultivating such renunciation. And the fifth stanza presents the measure, or criteria, of having generated true renunciation. These three aspects of the practice—its importance, the actual method, and the measure of success—should also be applied to the presentation of the altruistic awakening mind (*bodhichitta*) in subsequent verses. We read in the third stanza:

3. Without pure renunciation there is no way to pacify
   the yearning for the joys and fruits of samsara's ocean;
   since craving for existence chains us thoroughly,
   first search for true renunciation.

Now this expression "true renunciation" emphasizes the specific type of renunciation sought here. Even animals turn themselves

away from obvious painful experiences and are repulsed by such suffering. That is not true renunciation. Likewise, meditators who yearn
for birth in the form and formless realms may spurn attraction to
pleasurable and joyful sensations—the second level of suffering, the
suffering of change—in favor of a state of total neutrality. However,
that's also not true renunciation. The renunciation we are talking
about here is a thought that turns away from even the third level of
suffering, the suffering of pervasive conditioning. Here, you need to
have a deep-rooted recognition of our pervasive conditioning as a
form of suffering, and also the recognition that the root of this
conditioning is fundamental ignorance. So *true renunciation* is a state
of mind that genuinely and deeply aspires to freedom from bondage
to ignorance. This state of mind is founded on a reasoned understanding and also impelled by wisdom.

People sometimes misunderstand renunciation as being fed up
with life. When they struggle for success in the world and fail, running into all sorts of problems, they become discouraged and, out
of desperation, say they are renouncing everything. That's not the
kind of renunciation we are talking about. That is defeatism. True
renunciation is grounded in a deep understanding of the nature of
suffering and cyclic existence. In fact the mantra of Buddha Shakyamuni, *Om muni muni mahamuniye svaha*, invokes "the Able One, the
Great Able One." An enlightened being has great ability and a high
degree of confidence in being able to accomplish a goal. This is not
a naïve confidence or a naïve faith but one grounded in understanding and knowledge. Thus, true Buddhist renunciation is not
that of a dejected person who feels powerless and sighs, "I'm so
tired! Poor me!"

In this stanza it states "Since craving for existence chains us thoroughly...." This points to something we discussed before, how craving and grasping re-activates our karmic potentials and brings them to a fertile state, which then gives rise to another rebirth in cyclic existence. We spoke about how, if the karmic potential were not reactivated and heightened by craving and grasping, then rebirth would be impossible. The point here is that craving and the grasping, as extensions of ignorance, are what creates our rebirth. This is why when the scriptures list the attributes of a truly spiritual person, freedom from attachment is listed first, because attachment and craving are what bind us to cyclic existence.

For the actual method of cultivating true renunciation, we read:

> 4a–b.   From cultivating the attitude that this human life is so
> hard to find
> and we have no time to spare, preoccupations with this
> life will cease.

The point here is that, as we discussed in earlier chapters, a genuine aspiration to attain liberation will only arise on the basis of a profound understanding of the four noble truths, and this in turn comes from deeply contemplating and reflecting on the causal dynamics of taking birth within samsara. This suggests that in order to generate a genuine renunciation, the aspiration for liberation, a lot of reflection—a lot of thinking and contemplation—is required. It is obviously not enough to simply be born a human being. You need to apply your mind and apply your intelligence to engage with these thought processes deeply. Only then will true renunciation arise within you.

True renunciation may be difficult to realize as a human being, but it is near impossible for other types of beings to cultivate. From that perspective, we can see the tremendous value that our existence as human beings brings. And not only is human existence endowed with such capacity for reflection, but the opportunity it accords us to pursue such realizations is truly rare. In these ways, we can see the importance of reflecting on the value and the preciousness of human existence.

When we understand the approach of the systematic training in this manner, we will then appreciate what we find in Gampopa's *Jewel Ornament of Liberation,* where he says that the ground of our practice is buddha nature (*tathagatagarbha*)—the essence or seed of buddhahood that all beings possess. The theory of buddha nature states that we all possess the potential for buddhahood; we all possess the possibility of removing the pollutants of the mind and attaining the buddha's perfect wisdom mind. So this buddha nature, this innate potential for buddhahood, is really the ground, or foundation.

Based on this ground, certain conditions need to come together for our path to succeed. The internal condition that we need is birth as a human being. The external condition is meeting a qualified spiritual teacher. When these two conditions, internal and external, meet on the basis of the ground, which is buddha nature, then we will have the opportunity to gradually overcome and remove all the pollutants of the mind, from the most obvious to the most subtle. Again, we see why it is crucial to cherish the opportunity accorded to us by our human existence and make contemplation of the preciousness of human existence an important element of our practice. Similarly, since that external condition of meeting a qualified teacher is critical, it becomes very important to seek and rely upon a qualified teacher.

A QUALIFIED TEACHER

The qualifications of a teacher will differ depending on the context. For example, the monastic discipline texts present a set of qualities of a teacher, and if it is a question of taking precepts about ethical discipline, then you need to ensure the person you seek as your teacher possesses those basic qualifications outlined in the Vinaya texts. Similarly, texts on general Mahayana teachings also list specific qualifications of teachers. For example, Maitreya's *Ornament of Mahayana Sutras* lists ten such qualities of a Mahayana teacher.[40] And within the Vajrayana teachings the four classes of tantra each present specific attributes that are required of a qualified teacher. You need to ensure that you are familiar with the key qualities of a teacher and that the person you seek as your teacher possesses these qualities. For instance, a teacher should have ethical discipline, a peaceful mind, and knowledge of the scriptures. He or she would ideally have genuine insight into what he or she is teaching and, at the very least, be more advanced than the student with regard to the subject being taught. Until you have some conviction that the person you wish to take on as your teacher possesses these qualities, you need to subject him or her to scrutiny, examination. In the meantime, if you do need to take teachings, relate to him or her more as a colleague with whom you are engaging in dialogue and discussion but not as a teacher in the formal sense. Otherwise, there could be problems, as has happened in recent times. You need to be careful.

On the teacher's part, Tsongkhapa has stated emphatically in his *Great Treatise* that if one is not disciplined, it is simply not possible to induce discipline in others' minds.[41] If you have not disciplined your own mind, you cannot tame the minds of others. Therefore, those who aspire to teach and help others must first tame their own mind. Members of the Sangha who are wearing monastic robes and running Buddhist centers in particular need to ensure that they live up to the example of a genuine practitioner and member of the Buddha's order.

Then Tsongkhapa explains the process by which we need to discipline the mind. This process, he says, needs to be based on the general approach of the framework of the Buddha's path. As he explains, the "general framework" is the three higher trainings—the trainings in morality, meditation, and wisdom. It is on this basis that we must first discipline our own minds.[42]

Say one sets up a Buddhist center, and the center becomes merely a way of making a living. This is truly dangerous. Similarly, if a center becomes solely a vehicle for raising money, that too is not good. This reminds me of an autobiography of a Nyingma lama from Kongpo called Tselé Natsok Rangdröl. He was a monk and a great practitioner. In the autobiography, he mentions that in Tibet, the main way of getting from one place to another place was by riding a horse. He writes that, from a very young age, he decided to give up mounting horses out of compassion for the animals. He would always walk from place to place. Later on, he also gave up eating meat. Because he was a lama with a title, wherever he went many people—devotees—made offerings to him. He felt that in some sense, he was becoming a merchant of spiritual teaching. Thus he made a point of not accepting any offerings for the teachings that he gave. He set a truly remarkable example.

Several years ago, I began refusing any offering for the teachings I give. In the past, it had been customary to make offerings to me at the conclusion of a teaching, but I do not need any money for myself—I have nothing to spend it on. Previously, I would divide the offering up among various deserving projects and causes. When I did that, I would sometimes forget important projects, and people would feel left out and disappointed, thinking, "Oh, the Dalai Lama didn't give any to *us*, he gave it to *them*." It was becoming a chore, an unnecessary responsibility, and a headache, worrying about who should get the money. Thus I made it clear that I don't want to receive any offering and thereby end up with this extra burden. Instead the organizers should endeavor to keep the price of the tickets down so that more people can afford to benefit from these teachings. If people want to donate to different causes, they don't have to do it through me.

BENEFIT BEYOND THIS LIFE

So, we read earlier in the stanza that "this human life is so hard to find." This refers to the preciousness or the rarity of human existence mentioned above. Generally speaking, the greater the quality of something, the rarer its causes and conditions. Human existence is extremely rare, extremely difficult to assemble the causes for. Not only that, our lives are also transient, in that our deaths are certain; on top of that, the time when death will occur is unpredictable. In this way, we need to reflect upon the certainty of death and the unpredictability of its timing, and we also need to recognize that at the point of death, or after death, nothing but the Dharma practice we have done will benefit us.

As we saw in the discussion of the twelve links of dependent origination, consciousness acts as a repository for the potentials created by our past actions of body, speech, and mind. When such a karmic action is committed, the event ceases, but it leaves an imprint upon the consciousness. It is these imprints that are carried over across lives. When they meet the right conditions, the imprints are activated and heightened and bear their fruits.

Thus, when we refer to *Dharma* in saying that "only Dharma will benefit us after death," we are referring to the positive karmic potentials we have imprinted upon our consciousness. These positive karmic potentials can only be imprinted and cultivated by engaging in actions motivated by ethical or spiritual intention, whether that is an altruistic intention to help someone or an intention characterized by other positive qualities, such as renunciation or faith. Actions motivated by such positive intentions become positive karmic activity.

The Dharma that can benefit us after death is these positive karmic potentials, which we carry across to the next life. When we die, no matter how much wealth we may have amassed, none of it can be brought into the next life. No matter how famous we may be, that fame will not reach the next life. No matter how many good friends and loving family members we may have, none of them can be taken to the next life. The only thing taken to the next life is the karmic potentials we have imprinted on the consciousness, whether positive or negative.

Generally speaking, karmic actions are performed through our body, our speech, or our mind. Actions such as making prostrations, circumambulating holy places, and giving charity to the needy are bodily actions. Similarly, reciting mantras, making prayers, and so on, are Dharma activity of speech. Finally the Dharma activity of the mind includes positive thoughts like equanimity, compassion, faith, and the various realizations of the path. Among actions of body, speech, and mind, the first two are not the most important. The reason why is quite simple: an individual can engage both physically and verbally in what looks like a spiritual activity—prostrations, mantra recitation, and so on—while simultaneously harboring ill will, greed, or some other affliction; such actions of body and speech can coexist with a nonvirtuous activity. Therefore, the actions of body and speech are secondary—they are not the real Dharma practice.

The real Dharma practice is performed with the mind. Virtuous practices of the mind—such as cultivating loving-kindness and compassion, reflecting upon the transient nature of life, or contemplating selflessness—cannot coexist with a nonvirtuous state of mind. During the period that virtuous mental Dharma practices are actively transpiring, no negative activity can take place. That is why the Dharma action of mind is supreme; it is the genuine Dharma action.

Knowing this, it becomes very important to ensure the purity of our motivation. Often our motivation for practicing Dharma is tainted by worldly concerns, whether for longevity, wealth, good health, or worldly success. Of course if your aspiration for wealth or longevity is grounded in bodhichitta, the aspiration to attain buddhahood for the benefit of all sentient beings—if longevity or wealth are sought as a beneficial condition to further that ultimate goal—that is fine. On the other hand, if the aspiration for wealth or good health becomes your primary motive, then even if you are reciting mantras or performing tantric rites, it is nothing but mundane activity.

In fact, if a person propitiates the deity of wealth Jambala with the primary aim to become wealthy, it is open to question whether

Jambala will even grant their wishes. Jambala, a deity with a bulging belly, may look like a millionaire, but that he will grant that person a million is doubtful! I have mentioned several times to groups of Tibetans that if propitiating Jambala really made someone a millionaire, we should see quite a few Tibetan millionaires by now, which is not the case! On the other hand, we do see in other communities quite a few millionaires who have not propitiated Jambala but who have accumulated wealth through hard work. So it is very important that when we engage in spiritual activities that our motivation, our intention, is not tainted by worldly concerns.

THE SUFFERING OF SAMSARA

Next we read:

> **4c–d. By repeatedly contemplating the truth of karma and
>   samsaric suffering,
>   preoccupations with the next life will cease.**

"The truth of karma" here is the ineluctable nature of the law of karma. Broadly speaking, if you have created a particular karma, you will reap the fruit of that karma. The key point of contemplating samsaric suffering here is, as explained before, the recognition that as long as we remain chained to fundamental ignorance, there will be no room for lasting and true happiness. Seeing this, we come to recognize that cyclic existence is, by its very nature, flawed.

To understand how to contemplate the suffering of samsaric existence, we can bring the seventh stanza up here into the context of developing true renunciation:

> They [beings] are constantly swept away by four powerful
>   rivers;
> they're bound tightly with fetters of karma most difficult to
>   escape;
> they're trapped inside the iron mesh of self-grasping;
> they're enveloped in thick mists of ignorance;

In the text itself, these contemplations are presented in the context of generating compassion. Compassion and true renunciation are very similar; the difference is the focus of the contemplation—true renunciation relates to ourselves and our own suffering, while compassion relates to other sentient beings and their suffering. That is why, when cultivating true renunciation, it is helpful to bring these contemplations up and extend them to ourselves. How we do this is as follows.

We first reflect upon the fact that we are constantly being swept away by the four rivers. The "four rivers" here are birth, sickness, aging, and death. We are unrelentingly swept up in the powerful currents of these four rivers. As it says in the next line, while this is happening, we are tightly chained by the fetters of karma. Were we being swept away but were not bound, we'd have at least some hope of escape. But since our limbs are bound, then that hope of escape is even more remote.

In the discussion on the twelve links of dependent origination, we saw how aging and death arise when there is a birth. Birth, the eleventh link, arises from *becoming* or the heightened karmic potential, the tenth link. This heightened karmic potential arises when activated by craving and grasping. These in turn become possible only when there is the second link, volitional action—the karmic action that is committed. That, in turn, is motivated by fundamental ignorance, the first link. Without fundamental ignorance, the volitional act will not occur, and without the volitional act, then all the subsequent links will come to an end. We need to reflect upon how, bound by the links of this karmic chain, we are constantly swept up in this current of birth, sickness, aging, and death.

On top of that, we are trapped inside an iron-mesh cage of self-grasping. *Self-grasping* is the grasping at the self-existence of the person, grasping at our own personal existence as inherently real. This is also known as *egoistic grasping*. And while trapped in this cage, we are completely enveloped in a dense fog of ignorance, which here refers to the grasping at the inherent existence of phenomena.

This all points to the following situation: On the basis of grasping at phenomena as inherently real, the grasping at self—"I am"— arises. On the basis of this egoistic grasping, we create the karma. The karma then brings about a whole chain of events, such as birth, sickness, aging, and death. If you reflect in this manner, you will eventually realize that the cycle of existence, samsara, is near limitless—it has no discernable end. And in this trap of cyclic existence, we are endlessly tormented by the three types of sufferings. Thus we see that although Tsongkhapa expresses these reflections in the context of generating compassion for the suffering of others, the same verse can be brought up and applied to our own suffering as a way to cultivate true renunciation.

MEASURE OF TRUE RENUNCIATION

Then the next stanza presents the measure of having generated true renunciation. We read:

5. Having habituated your mind in this way, when not even
   an instant
   of admiration arises for the riches of cyclic existence
   and the thought aspiring for liberation arises day and
   night,
   at this point true renunciation has arisen.

The point is that when you see from the depths of your heart
that it is possible to eradicate ignorance, then developing a genuine
aspiration for liberation becomes far more realistic.

The approach here really reflects the general Buddhist approach
we have spoken about. When we speak of the approach of the
Buddhist path, we can divide it into two approaches. One is a very
general approach that reflects the basic framework of the Buddhist
path. The other one would be an approach suited to a particular
individual or a particular context. The presentation here is in accordance with Nagarjuna's *Fundamental Stanzas on the Middle Way,* whose
intended audience and practitioner is someone with a higher mental faculty. This presentation reflects the general approach of the
Mahayana path, wherein the practitioner cultivates a deep understanding of the nature of liberation and, therefore, a deep understanding of emptiness *prior* to developing a genuine renunciation.
Based on his or her understanding of emptiness, the practitioner
recognizes that liberation is possible, and that recognition induces
a genuine aspiration for such liberation.

Similarly, a bodhisattva practitioner, before developing genuine
bodhichitta, needs first of all some understanding of the nature of
the enlightenment that is being sought, and for this, understanding
emptiness is crucial. It is conceivable that this approach for intelligent

practitioners may not be suitable for specific individuals, but the true renunciation—the aspiration to attain liberation—realized by such a practitioner does not contain a distinct idea of what that liberation consists of. Their idea is kind of fuzzy, but it is nonetheless powerful enough for them to develop a genuine aspiration for liberation or for buddhahood.

BODHICHITTA, THE AWAKENING MIND

The second principal aspect of the path, bodhichitta, is presented beginning in the sixth stanza. First is the presentation of why it is important to develop bodhichitta, or awakening mind. We read,

6. Such renunciation, too, if not sustained
    by pure awakening mind, will not become a cause
    of the perfect bliss of unexcelled enlightenment;
    therefore, O intelligent ones, generate the excellent
    awakening mind.

As this states, if our true renunciation is not accompanied by bodhichitta, then we will not be able to attain complete enlightenment.

Then, the seventh stanza, along with the first two lines of the eighth, presents the actual method for cultivating the awakening mind. As we saw above, when these lines are read in relation to our own situation, they give rise to true renunciation. When read in the context of other sentient beings' suffering, they engender great compassion within us.

7. They're constantly swept away by four powerful rivers;
    they're bound tightly with fetters of karma most difficult
        to escape;
    they're trapped inside the iron mesh of self-grasping;
    they're enveloped in thick mists of ignorance.

8a–b. They take birth within cyclic existence that has no end,
        where they're endlessly tormented by the three
            sufferings.

Then, in the final two lines of the eighth stanza, we read:

8c–d. By reflecting on all your mothers who suffer such
            conditions,
        Please generate the supreme awakening mind.

The method for generating compassion is first to recognize
the nature of suffering. We discussed this above in the context of
our own suffering, and now we apply the same analysis to the suffering of others in order to grasp the nature of their pain and
develop the compassionate wish to free them of it. Here
Tsongkhapa uses the word *mother*, "all your mothers." to refer to
other sentient beings. You call them your mothers to encourage
within you a deep sense of intimacy with them and a genuine concern for their welfare.

These two factors—understanding the nature of suffering and
a feeling of closeness with other sentient beings—become the basis
to develop a genuine desire to secure others' welfare. When this compassionate wish to relieve the suffering of others is extended to all

beings unconditionally, then you have realized what is called *great compassion,* which then leads to a sense of commitment to bringing about others' welfare by yourself, the *extraordinary altruistic resolve* has arisen in you. And when you develop a genuine, spontaneous aspiration for buddhahood, full enlightenment, in order to accomplish this aim, then you have generated bodhichitta, the awakening mind. Bodhichitta is, as explained earlier, the altruistic awakening mind that is endowed with these two aspirations—the aspiration to bring about others' welfare, and to that end, the aspiration to attain enlightenment.

The measure of having generated bodhichitta can be inferred on the basis of the measure of having generated renunciation we discussed earlier. In short, you have attained bodhichitta when the altruistic wish for enlightenment has become the motivating force behind all your actions of body, speech, and mind.

Meditating on emptiness

Next, the importance of meditating on emptiness is explained in the ninth stanza, where we read:

9. Without the wisdom realizing the ultimate nature,
   even if you gain familiarity with renunciation and
      awakening mind,
   you will not be able to cut the root of samsaric
      existence;
   strive then in the means of realizing dependent
      origination.

We've already examined emptiness quite extensively in the chapters on Nagarjuna's *Fundamental Stanzas on the Middle Way,* and so we need not explore that again here at length.

In the next stanza, we find the true understanding of what emptiness means. We read that,

> 10. When with respect to all phenomena of samsara and
>   nirvana,
>   you can see that causes and effects never deceive their
>   laws;
>   and when you dissolve the focus of objectification,
>   you enter the path that pleases the buddhas.

If you have dissolved all appearances of true existence without violating the laws of cause and effect and the world of conventional reality, then you have found the true understanding of emptiness and entered "the path that pleases the buddhas."

We then read:

> 11. As long as the two understandings—of appearance,
>   which is undeceiving dependent origination,
>   and emptiness devoid of all theses—remain separate,
>   you will not have realized the intent of the Sage.

As long as your understanding of the world of appearance, or conventional reality, and your understanding of the world of emptiness, the ultimate nature, remain at odds with each other—when they remain separate and undermine each other—you have not fully understand the intent of the Buddha.

Then, Tsongkhapa writes further,

12. However, when, not in alternation but all at once,
      the instant you see that dependent origination is
         undeceiving,
      the entire object of grasping at certainty is dismantled,
      then your analysis of the view has fully matured.

This presents the criteria for having fully understood emptiness. When you understand emptiness in terms of dependent origination and you understand dependent origination in terms of
emptiness, like two sides of the same coin, when you have completely negated inherent existence with no residue left behind, then
your realization is complete. Normally, when we perceive things in
our day-to-day experience, we see them as possessing some objective
intrinsic reality, and then we follow after that appearance. But once
you truly understand emptiness, then the moment you perceive a
thing, that appearance itself is adequate to instantly trigger your
understanding of emptiness. Instead of immediately grasping on to
a thing's intrinsic reality, now you are instantly mindful that, "Yes,
it appears this object is intrinsically real, but that is not so." The
appearance itself automatically induces your understanding of
emptiness. When that happens, then you have completed your
process of analysis.

Then in the next stanza we read:

13. Furthermore, when appearance dispels the extreme of
      existence
      and emptiness dispels the extreme of nonexistence,

and you understand how emptiness arises as cause and
   effect,
you will never be captivated by views grasping at
   extremes.

This stanza echoes Chandrakirti in his *Entering the Middle Way*
(*Madhyamakavatara*), where he writes that, just as reflections, echoes,
and so on are empty of any substantial reality and yet still appear
though the meeting of conditions, phenomena—form, feeling, and
so on—though devoid of intrinsic existence, arise from within
emptiness with their own characteristics and identities.[43] The point
is that emptiness itself acts like a cause for the flourishing of the
world of multiplicity; all phenomena are in some sense manifestations of emptiness—a kind of a play that arises from the sphere of
emptiness. This stanza echoes those lines from Chandrakirti's text.

The final stanza is a conclusion, which urges the practitioner to
engage in these teachings. Tsongkhapa writes:

14. Once you have understood as they are
     the essentials of the three principal aspects of the path,
     O son, seek solitude, and by enhancing your powers of
        perseverance,
     swiftly accomplish your ultimate aim.

This has been a very brief explanation, based on the *Three Principal Aspects of the Path*, of how to bring all the points we discussed in
the previous chapters to bear on the sphere of actual practice.

CULTIVATING UNDERSTANDING

If you are serious about Dharma practice, it is important to cultivate a good understanding of the teachings. First of all, it is important to read the texts. The more texts you read—the more you expand the scope of your learning and reading—the greater the resources you will find for your own understanding and practice. When, as a result of deep study and contemplation on what you have learned, as related to your personal understanding, you reach a point on each topic when you have developed a deep conviction that this is how it is, that's an indication you have attained what is called the understanding derived through contemplation or reflection. Before that, all your understanding will have been intellectual understanding, but at that point it shifts. Then you have to cultivate familiarity, make it into part of your daily habit. The more you cultivate familiarity, the more it will become experiential.

Of course in relation to the path there are two aspects: method and wisdom. Generally speaking, it is easier to understand the method aspect of the path, and easier to develop a deeper conviction about it as well. It evokes strong, powerful emotions. But even with the wisdom aspect of the path, although the initial stages of cultivating understanding and deep conviction are more difficult, once you gain profound conviction, then you can experience powerful feelings and emotions.

However, you should not have short-term expectations that something like this will necessarily be achieved within a few years. Regarding the duration of practice it is important to seek inspiration from statements in the scriptures. They explain that it takes three innumerable eons to achieve full enlightenment. Also Shantideva, in his *Guide to the Bodhisattva's Way of Life* (*Bodhicharyavatara*), says that we should pray that as long as space remains and sentient beings remain, may I too remain to dispel the sufferings of sentient beings.[44] Reflecting on these kinds of sentiments will give you strength and inspiration. If you train your mind in such a manner, although your body may remain the same as before, your mind will change and transform. The result is happiness. Whether the outcome will bring benefit to others depends on many factors and external conditions. But as far as our own experience is concerned, the benefit is definitely there.

PRACTICE THE PROFOUND

Each morning after you wake up, try to shape your thinking in beneficial ways before you begin your day. You can think, for instance, "May my body, my speech, and my mind be used in a more compassionate way so that they become a service to others." This is something I usually do. It makes life more meaningful. Likewise, examine your mind in the evening before you go to bed. Review the way you spent your day and check whether it was worthwhile. Even for nonreligious people, I believe this is a valuable method to create a more meaningful life, so that when you arrive at the end of life, you do not feel remorse or regret. You may be sad because you are now departing from this world, but at the same time, you have some satisfaction from having lived your life in a meaningful way.

One particularly helpful habit to develop is the habit of watching your own thought processes, observing what occurs in your mind so you are not totally immersed in it. Usually when we develop anger, for instance, our whole mind or self seems to become anger. But that is just an appearance. With some experience, you can learn to step back when anger develops. It is enormously helpful to be able to recognize the destructiveness of a negative emotion right in the moment it develops. This is of course very difficult, but through training you can do it. Then, when you have some perspective on your own anger, you look at your anger and, immediately, the intensity of it is reduced. It works the same way for attachment, sadness, pride, and so on. Through training and habituation, cultivating a daily habit, this is possible.

These are also ways to extend human value outward, extending from a single person to family members, and from each family member to their friends. That is the way to transform family, community, eventually nation, and then humanity. If each person cultivates his or her mind, the effects will spread and lead to a better world. After I pass away, after forty or fifty years, perhaps a better world will come, but if you want that, you must start working for it from today, from right now.

That is what I want to share with you.

Appendix 1:
Three Principal Aspects of the Path

Jé Tsongkhapa

(Tibetan title: *Lam gyi gtso bo rnam pa gsum*)

Homage to the most venerable teachers!

1. I will explain here to the best of my ability
   the essential points of all the scriptures of the Conqueror,
   the path acclaimed by all excellent bodhisattvas,
   the gateway for fortunate ones aspiring for liberation.

2. Those who are not attached to the joys of cyclic existence,
   who strive to make meaningful this life of leisure and
       opportunities
   and who place their trust in the path that pleases the
       conquerors—
   O fortunate ones, listen with an open heart.

3. Without pure renunciation there is no way to pacify
   the yearning for the joys and fruits of samsara's ocean;

149

since craving for existence chains us thoroughly,
first search for true renunciation.

4. From cultivating the attitude that this human life is so
        hard to find
    and we have no time to spare, preoccupations with this life
        will cease;
    by repeatedly contemplating the truth of karma and
        samsaric suffering,
    preoccupations with the next life will cease.

5. Having habituated your mind in this way, when not even
        an instant
    of admiration arises for the riches of cyclic existence
    and the thought aspiring for liberation arises day and
        night,
    at this point true renunciation has arisen.

6. Such renunciation, too, if not sustained
    by pure awakening mind, will not become a cause
    of the perfect bliss of unexcelled enlightenment;
    therefore, O intelligent ones, generate the excellent
        awakening mind.

7. They're constantly swept away by four powerful rivers;
    they're bound tightly with fetters of karma most
        difficult to escape;
    they're trapped inside the iron mesh of self-grasping;
    they're enveloped in thick mists of ignorance.

8. They take birth within cyclic existence that has no end,
    where they're endlessly tormented by the three sufferings.
    By reflecting on all your mothers who suffer such
        conditions,
    please generate the supreme awakening mind.

9. Without the wisdom realizing the ultimate nature,
    even if you gain familiarity with renunciation and
        awakening mind,
    you will not be able to cut the root of samsaric existence;
    strive then in the means of realizing dependent origination.

10. When with respect to all phenomena of samsara and
        nirvana,
    you can see that causes and effects never deceive their laws;
    and when you dissolve the focus of objectification,
    you enter the path that pleases the buddhas.

11. As long as the two understandings—of appearance,
    which is undeceiving dependent origination,
    and emptiness devoid of all theses—remain separate,
    you will not have realized the intent of the Sage.

12. However, when, not in alternation but all at once,
    the instant you see that dependent origination is
        undeceiving
    the entire object of grasping at certainty is dismantled,
    then your analysis of the view has fully matured.

13. Furthermore, when appearance dispels the extreme of
        existence
    and emptiness dispels the extreme of nonexistence,
    and you understand how emptiness arises as cause and
        effect,
    you will never be captivated by views grasping at extremes.

14. Once you have understood as they are
    the essentials of the three principal aspects of the path,
    O son, seek solitude, and by enhancing your powers of
        perseverance,
    swiftly accomplish your ultimate aim.

This advice was given by the monk Lobsang Drakpai Pal to Ngawang Drakpa, a leading person of Tsakho region.

Appendix 2:
Praise to Seventeen Nalanda Masters[45]

His Holiness the Dalai Lama

Herein is a praise to seventeen Nalanda masters entitled "A Sun Illuminating the Threefold Faith."

1. Born from great compassion aspiring to help all beings,
    god of gods, you have attained the savior's state of
        abandonment and realization
    and you guide beings through the discourse of dependent
        origination.
    O able one, the sun of speech, I bow my head to you.

2. I bow at your feet, O Nagarjuna, most skilled in elucidating
    suchness free of elaborations—the essence of the *Mother of
        Conquerors* sutras—
    through the reasoning of dependent origination.
    In accord with Conqueror's prophecy, you initiated the
        Middle Way.

3. I bow to your principal son, bodhisattva Aryadeva,
   most learned and realized,
   who has crossed the ocean of Buddhist and non-Buddhist
       philosophies,
   and is the crown jewel among those who uphold
       Nagarjuna's treatises.

4. I bow to you, O Buddhapalita, who has reached
   the supreme adept's state and who has clearly elucidated
   Noble [Nagarjuna's] intent, the final meaning of
       dependent origination,
   the profound point of existence as mere designation and
       as mere name.

5. I bow to you, O master Bhavaviveka, most accomplished
       pandita,
   you initiated the philosophical tradition wherein while
       negating
   such extremes as the arising of truly existing things,
   one upholds commonly verified knowledge as well as
       external reality.

6. I bow to you, O Chandrakirti, who disseminated all the
       paths of sutra and tantra.
   You are most skilled in teaching the profound and the vast
       aspects of the Middle Way—
   the union of appearance and emptiness dispelling the two
       extremes—
   by means of dependent origination that is mere
       conditionality.

7. I bow to you, O bodhisattva Shantideva, most skilled
    at revealing to the assembly of most-fortunate spiritual
        trainees
    the excellent path of compassion that is most wondrous
    through lines of reasoning most profound and vast.

8. I bow to you, O master abbot Shantarakshita, who initiated
    the tradition of Nondual Middle Way in accordance with
        trainee's mental disposition.
    You're versed in the reasoning modes of both Middle Way
        and valid cognition,
    and you disseminated the Conqueror's teaching in the
        Land of Snows.

9. I bow at your feet, O Kamalashila, you who, having
        explained excellently
    the stages of meditation of the Middle Way view free of
        elaborations
    and the union of tranquility and insight in accordance
        with sutra and tantra,
    flawlessly elucidated the Conqueror's teaching in the Land
        of Snows.

10. I bow at your feet, O Asanga, you who, sustained by
        Maitreya,
    were versed in disseminating excellently all Mahayana
        scriptures
    and taught the vast path and who, in accord with the
        Conqueror's prophecy,
    initiated the tradition of Mind Only.

11. I bow at your feet, O master Vasubandhu, you who, while
      upholding
     the systems of the seven Abhidharma treatises as well as
      Nonduality,
     clarified the tenets of Vaibhashika, Sautrantika, and
      Mind Only.
     Foremost among learned ones, you're renowned as a second
      Omniscient One.

12. I bow at your feet, O Dignaga, the logician,
     you who, in order to present the Buddha's way through
      evidence-based reasoning,
     opened hundredfold gateways of valid cognition
     and offered as a gift to the world the eyes of critical
      intelligence.

13. I bow at your feet, O Dharmakirti, you who, understanding
     all the essential points of both Buddhist and non-Buddhist
      epistemology,
     brought conviction in all the profound and vast paths of
      Sautrantika and Mind Only by means of reasoning;
     you were most versed in teaching the excellent Dharma.

14. I bow at your feet, O Vimuktisena, you who lit the lamp
      that illuminates
     the meaning of the *Ornament* treatise wherein the themes
      of *Perfection of Wisdom*

stemming from Asanga and his brother were expounded
in accord with Middle Way view free of existence and
nonexistence.

15. I bow to you, O master Haribhadra, who were prophesized
by the Conqueror as expounder of the meaning of the
Mother, the perfection of wisdom.
You elucidated the excellent treatise on the perfection of
wisdom, the three mothers,
in perfect accord with the instruction of the savior
Maitreya.

16. I bow at your feet, O Gunaprabha, most excellent in both
integrity and scholarship, who, having excellently distilled
the intent
of one hundred thousand disciplinary teachings,
expounded the individual liberation vows
flawlessly according to the tradition of Sarvastivada
school.

17. I bow at your feet, O Shakyaprabha, supreme upholder
of discipline,
who reigned over the treasury of jewels of the three
trainings.
In order to disseminate the stainless discipline teachings
for a long time,
you excellently expounded the meaning of the vast
[discipline] treatises.

18. I bow to you, O master Atisha, you who, having taught
    all the profound and vast traditions related to the words
        of the Buddha
    within the framework of the path of the persons of three
        capacities,
    were the most kind master disseminating the Buddha's
        teaching in the Land of Snows.

19. Having thus praised these most learned ornaments of the
        world,
    the excellent sources of wondrous and insightful teachings,
    may I, with a mind unwavering and pure,
    be blessed so that my mind becomes ripened and free.

20. By understanding the two truths, the way things exist,
    I will ascertain how, through the four truths, we enter and
        exit samsara;
    I will make firm the faith in the Three Jewels that is born
        of valid reason.
    May I be blessed so that the root of the liberating path is
        firmly established within me.

21. May I be blessed to perfect the training in renunciation—
    an aspiration for liberation, the total pacification of
        suffering and its origin—
    as well as in an uncontrived awakening mind that is
        rooted in
    an infinite compassion that wishes to protect all sentient
        beings.

22. May I be blessed so that I may easily develop conviction
     in all the paths
   pertaining to the profound points of the Perfection and
     Vajra Vehicles,
   by engaging in study, reflection, and meditation on the
     meaning
   of the treatises of the great trailblazers.[46]

23. May I, in life after life, obtain excellent embodiments that
     support
   the three trainings and make contributions to the teaching
     that equal the great trailblazers
   in upholding and disseminating the teaching of scripture
     and realization
   through engaging in exposition and meditative practice.

24. May the members of all spiritual communities spend
     their time
   in learning, reflection, and meditation.
   Through the proliferation of sublime masters who shun
     wrong livelihood,
   may the great face of the earth be beautified throughout
     all time.

25. Through their power, may I traverse all the paths of sutra
     and tantra
   and attain the conquerors' omniscience,
   characterized by spontaneous realization of the two
     purposes.

> May I work for the welfare of sentient beings as long as
> space remains.

COLOPHON

Thus, with respect to the profound and vast aspects of the excellent Dharma taught by the Blessed Buddha, these great masters of India, the land of the noble ones, referred to in the above lines composed excellent treatises that opened the eyes of intelligence of numerous discerning individuals. These writings survive without degeneration to this day—now approaching 2,550 years [following the Buddha's passing]—still serving as treatises for study, critical reflection, and meditation. Therefore, remembering the kindness of these learned masters, I aspire with unwavering devotion to follow in their footsteps.

Today, in an age when science and technology have reached a most advanced stage, we are incessantly preoccupied with mundane concerns. In such an age, it is crucial that we who follow the Buddha acquire faith in his teaching on the basis of genuine understanding. It is with an objective mind endowed with a curious skepticism that we should engage in careful analysis and seek the reasons.

Then, on the basis of seeing the reasons, we engender a faith that is accompanied by wisdom. For this, the excellent treatises on the profound and vast aspects [of the path] by the great masters, such as the well-known six ornaments and two supreme masters,[47] as well as Buddhapalita, Vimuktisena, and so on, remain indispensable. Even in the past there was a tradition to have paintings of the six ornaments and the two supreme masters made on thangka scrolls. To these I have added nine more lineage masters of the profound and vast aspects of the path, commissioning a thangka painting of seventeen great panditas of the glorious Nalanda Monastery.

In conjunction with this, I wanted to compose a prayer that expresses my heartfelt reverence for these most excellent learned beings, and in addition, some interested individuals and spiritual colleagues also encouraged me to write such a piece. Thus this supplication to seventeen masters of glorious Nalanda entitled "Sun Illuminating the Threefold Faith" was written by the Buddhist monk Tenzin Gyatso, someone who has found an uncontrived faith in the excellent writings of these great masters and sits among the last rows of individuals engaged in the study of these excellent works.

This was composed and completed at Thekcken Choeling, Dharamsala, Kangara District, Himachal Pradesh, India, in the 2548th year of Buddha's parinirvana according to the Theravada system, on the first day of the eleventh month of Iron-Snake year in the seventeenth Rabjung cycle of the Tibetan calendar, that is December 15, 2001, of the Common Era.

May goodness prevail!

Notes

1. "Recognizing My Mother," in *Songs of Spiritual Experience* (Boston: Shambhala Publications, 2000), p. 112.

2. For a more extensive explanation of the four noble truths by the Dalai Lama, see his *Four Noble Truths* (London: Thorsons, 1997). This short book has been reprinted in its entirety in *The Heart of the Buddha's Path* (London: Thorsons, 1999).

3. To my knowledge, no source sutra for this verse has been found in the Tibetan canon; however, the passage is said to exist in the Pali canon.

4. *Mulamadhamakakarika*, 24:8ab.

5. *Abhisamayalamkara*, 1:21ab.

6. For an extensive teaching on the twelve links of dependent origination by the Dalai Lama, see his *Meaning of Life: Buddhist Perspectives on Cause and Effect* (Boston: Wisdom Publications, 1993).

7. *Pratityasamutpadahridayakarika*, verse 2.

8. The translation of Nagarjuna's text provided here is based on Jay Garfield's translation found in his *The Fundamental Wisdom of the Middle Way* with substantial modifications. These changes have been introduced to reflect my own reading of the text as well as to suit His Holiness's commentary on the specific stanzas of Nagarjuna's root text.

9. Here His Holiness is alluding to a standard classification of the objects of knowledge into the three categories of evident facts, hidden facts (which can be inferred on the basis of observed facts), and extremely hidden facts. This latter includes, among others, the facts about the minute details of the workings of karma.

10. Gungthang Jampaiyang, a.k.a. Könchok Tenpai Drönmé (1762–1823), was a prolific author and a revered teacher. In 1792, Gungthang Rinpoché became the abbot of Tashikhyil Monastery, a major Geluk institution in northeastern Tibet founded in 1709 by Jamyang Shepa. Tashikhyil often goes by the name Labrang.

11. *Mahayanasutralamkara,* 21:8.

12. This is a reference to the sutra entitled *Pratityasamutpadadivibhanganirdeshasutra* (Tohoku canon 211, sutras, vol. *tsa,* p. 223, line 6).

13. *Chatuhshatakashastrakarika,* 14:25.

14. *Three Principal Aspects of the Path,* v. 7cd. See His Holiness's commentary on this text in chapter 5 of this book.

15. *Mulamadhyamakakarika,* 24:18ab.

16. *Chatuhshatakashastrakarika,* 8:5cd.

17. *The Great Treatise on the Stages of the Path to Enlightenment,* vol. 1, trans. by the Lamrim Chenmo Translation Committee (Ithaca NY: Snow Lion, 2000), p. 306. The "field's power" here refers to sacred objects, such as enlightened beings and their reliquaries, that have such powerful liberating energy that actions of faith performed in relation to them—even if such actions are not informed by the view of emptiness—plant the seeds of liberation in the mind.

18. This first type of karma is very different from the type of karma that constitutes the second link of the twelve links in that this karma by definition never propels a rebirth.

19. *Ratnavali,* 1:35.

20. These are frequently referred to by the terms *selflessness of persons* and *selflessness of phenomena.*

21. *Ratnavali,* 1:80–81b.

22. *Clear Words (Prasannapada),* 22.

23. *Chatuhshatakashastrakarika,* 14:25. This stanza was cited above on page 57.

24. *Pramanavarttika,* 2:193.

25. Within the twofold division of the object of negation—the object of negation of the path and the object of negation of reasoning—elaboration in the form of grasping at true existence is mostly the object of negation of the path. Such an elaboration is a mental state, which is why it is said here that it is the *realization* of emptiness, and not emptiness itself, that leads to cessation.

26. Nagarjuna's six analytic works are *Fundamental Stanzas on the Middle Way (Mulamadhyamakakarika), Sixty Stanzas of Reasoning (Yuktishashtika), Seventy Stanzas on Emptiness (Shunyatasaptati), Finely Woven Thread (Vaidalyasutra), Refutation of Objections (Vigrahavyavartani),* and *Precious Garland (Ratnavali).* The last of these is the text that His Holiness did not receive a transmission of from Khunu Rinpoché.

27. *Madhyamakavatara,* 6:121. "Tirthikas" here refer to the upholders of non-Buddhist classical Indian philosophical schools.

28. E.g., *Mulamadhyamakakarika,* 13:7. "If even a trifle were not empty,/ emptiness, too, would possess a trifle of existence./ Since not even a trifle that is not empty exists,/ how could emptiness exist?"

29. *Mulamadhyamakakarika,* 13:8: "The conquerors have said/ that emptiness frees from all views./ So those who view emptiness [to be real]/ are beyond repair, they've taught."

30. *Yuktishashtika*, 51. A complete English translation of this work can be found at http://www.tibetanclassics.org/Jinpa_Translation.html.

31. *Mulamadhyamakakarika*, 1:1.

32. *Root Verses on Indian Philosophies*, chap. 13:1. "Through both sutra and tantra, afflictive obscurations can cease./ Though the highest object is presented [in the sutras], the highest subject remains hidden;/ Though the chief pollutant is presented, the highest antidote remains hidden;/ The subtlest knowledge-obscuration is cleansed through tantra, not sutra." The full text of Jamyang Shepa's verses in English translation can be found at http://www.tibetanclassics.org/Jinpa_Translation.html.

33. The "eight kinds of persons" is a reference to the preceding verse: the four who reap the fruits and the four who enter the path. The four fruits are the fruits of the stream-enterer, the once-returner, the non-returner, and the arhat. The four who enter the path are those on the paths to reaping one of these fruits.

34. "Prasangika" refers to a subset among the interpreters of Nagarjuna's philosophy of emptiness, which include principally, the Indian masters Buddhapalita (ca. fifth century), Candrakirti (seventh century) and Shantideva (eighth century), the latter being the author of the famed *Guide to the Bodhisattva's Way of Life* (*Bodhicaryavatara*). For a detailed exposition by the Dalai Lama of the crucial ninth chapter of Shantideva's *Guide to the Bodhisattva's Way of Life*, which presents the teaching on emptiness, see *Practicing Wisdom* (Boston: Wisdom Publications, 2005).

35. Tohoku canon 156, sutras, vol. *pha*, p. 230b.

36. *Praise to Dependent Origination*, 19. The full text of this praise in English translation can be found at http://www.tibetanclassics.org/Jinpa_Translation.html.

37. His Holiness's own commentary on Longchenpa's *Mind at Ease* can be

found in *Mind in Comfort and Ease: The Vision of Enlightenment in the Great Perfection* (Boston: Wisdom Publications, 2007).

38. *Chatuhshatakashastrakarika*, 8:15.

39. An English translation of the *Lamrim Chenmo* was published in three volumes as *The Great Treatise on the Stages of the Path to Enlightenment* (Ithaca, NY: Snow Lion, 2000–2004). A translation of the middle-length work is forthcoming from Wisdom Publications. And a translation of the short lamrim work can be found at http://www.tibetanclassics.org/Jinpa_Translation.html. For His Holiness's commentary on this short lamrim, based on the Third Dalai Lama's *Essence of Refined Gold*, see H. H. The Dalai Lama, *The Path to Enlightenment*, trans. and ed. by Glenn Mullin (Ithaca, NY: Snow Lion, 1995).

40. *Mahayanasutralamkara*, 17:10. The ten qualities Maitreya lists are (1) discipline, (2) serenity, (3) thorough pacification, (4) more qualities than one's students, (5) energy, (6) a wealth of scriptural knowledge, (7) loving concern, (8) a thorough knowledge of reality, (9) skill in instructing disciples, and (10) freedom from despair. For a detailed explanation of each of these ten qualities, see Tsongkhapa's *The Great Treatise on the Stages of the Path to Enlightenment*, vol. 1, pp. 70–75.

41. *The Great Treatise*, vol. 1, p. 71.

42. Ibid.

43. *Madhyamakavatara*, 6:37.

44. *Bodhicharyavatara*, 10:55.

45. The translation of this supplication was done specially for this volume. An earlier translation of the prayer undertaken by Geshe Lhakdor Lobsang Jordan and edited by Jeremy Russell was published under the title *Illuminating the Threefold Faith: An Invocation of the Seventeen Scholarly Adepts of Glorious Nalanda* by Central Institute of Higher

Tibetan Studies, Sarnath, in 2006. This is a multilingual edition of the prayer that includes, in addition to Tibetan original and English, Sanskrit and Hindi translations of the text.

46. Literally, the "great charioteers" (*shing rta chen po*). This is a reference to Nagarjuna, the founder of the Middle Way school, and Asanga, the founder of the Mind Only school.

47. The six ornaments are Aryadeva, Vasubandhu, Nagarjuna, Asanga, Dignaga, and Dharmakirti. The two supreme masters are Gunaprabha and Shakyaprabha.

Bibliography

Note: For the benefit of those who wish to consult the original texts we have provided the Sanskrit and the Tibetan titles of the classical Buddhist texts. "Toh" stands for Tohoku and the numbers represent the catalogue entries of the Dergé edition of *Kangyur* (canonical scriptures) and *Tengyur* (commentarial treaties) in *A Complete Catalogue of the Tibetan Buddhist Canons*, edited by Prof. Hekuji Ui, Japan: Sendai, 1934.

Aryadeva. *Four Hundred Stanzas on the Middle Way* (*Chatuhshatakashastrakarika*). (Tib. *dbu ma bzhi brgya pa*; Toh 3846, Tengyur, *dbu ma*, vol. *tsha*.) An English translation of this text together with Gyaltsap Je's commentary exists under the title *Yogic Deeds of the Bodhisattvas* (Ithaca: Snow Lion, 1994).

Chandrakirti. *Entering the Middle Way* (*Madhyamakavatara*). (Tib. *dbu ma la 'jug pa*; Toh 3861, Tengyur, *dbu ma*, vol. *ha*.) English translations of this text can be found in C.W. Huntington, Jr.'s *The Emptiness of Emptiness* (Honolulu: University of Hawaii, 1989) and Candrakirti and Mipham's *Introducing the Middle Way* (Boston: Shambhala, 2005).

——————— . *Clear Words* (*Prasannapada*). (Tib. *dbu ma rtsa ba'i 'grel pa tshig gsal ba*; Toh 3860, Tengyur, *dbu ma*, vol. *dza*).

Chankya Rolpai Dorje (1717–86). "Recognizing My Mother" in Thupten Jinpa and Jas Elsner (edited) *Songs of Spiritual Experience*. Boston: Shambhala Publications, 2000.

Dharmakirti. *Commentary on "Valid Cognition"* (*Pramanavarttika*). (Tib. *tshad ma rnam 'grel*; Toh 4210, Tengyur, *tshad ma*, vol. *ce*.)

His Holiness the Dalai Lama. *Four Noble Truths*. Translated by Thupten Jinpa. London: Thorsons, 1997.

————— . *Meaning of Life: Buddhist Perspectives on Cause and Effect.* Translated and edited by Jeffrey Hopkins. Boston: Wisdom Publications, 1993.

————— . *Mind in Comfort and Ease: The Vision of Enlightenment in the Great Perfection.* Boston: Wisdom Publications, 2007.

————— . *Practicing Wisdom.* Translated and edited by Geshe Thupten Jinpa. Boston: Wisdom Publications, 2005.

————— . *The Path to Enlightenment.* Translated by Glenn Mullin. Ithaca, NY: Snow Lion Publications, 1995.

Jamyang Shepa. *Root Verses on Indian Philosophies* (*grub mtha' rtsa ba*). English translation of this text is available at http://www.tibetanclassics.org/ Jinpa_Translation.html.

Maitreya. *Ornament of Clear Realization* (*Abhisamayalamkara*). (Tib. *mngon rtogs rgyan*; Toh 3786, Tengyur, *shes phyin*, vol. *ka*.)

————— . *Ornament of Mahayana Sutras* (*Mahayanasutralamkara*). (Tib. *theg pa chen po mdo sde'i rgyan*; Toh 4020, Tengyur, *sems tsam*, vol. *phi*.) An English translation of this text together with Vasubhandu's commentary is available under the title *The Universal Vehicle Discourse Literature* (New York: American Institute of Buddhist Studies, 2004).

Nagarjuna. *Fundamental Wisdom of the Middle Way* (*Mulamadhyamakakarika*). A lucid English translation of this text can be found in Jay Garfield's *Fundamental Wisdom of the Middle Way* (New York: Oxford University Press, 1995).

————— . *Sixty Stanzas of Reasoning* (*Yuktishashtika*). An English translation of this text can be found at http://www.tibetanclassics. org/Jinpa_Translation.html.

——————— . *The Precious Garland* (*Ratnavali*). For an English translation of this text by John Dunne and Sara McClintock, see *The Precious Garland* (Boston: Wisdom Publications, 1997).

——————— . *Exposition of the Essence of Dependent Origination* (*Pratityasamutpadahridayakarika*). (Tib. *rten cing 'brel bar 'byung ba'i snying po'i rnam par bshad pa*; Toh 3837, Tengyur, *dbu ma*, vol. *tsa*.)

Presentation of the First and [the Other] Divisions of Dependent Origination Sutra (*Pratityasamutpadadivibhanganirdeshasutra*). (Tib. *rten cing 'brel bar byung ba dang po dang rnam par dbye ba bstan pa*; Toh 211, Kangyur, *mdo sde*, vol. *tsa*.)

Questions of the Naga King Anavatapta (*Anavatapatanagarajapariprccha*). (Tib. *klu'i rgyal po ma dros pas zhus pa'i mdo*; Toh 156, Kangyur, *mdo sde*, vol. *pha*.)

Shantideva. *Guide to the Bodhisattva's Way of Life* (*Bodhicaryavatara*). Toh 3871, *dbu ma*, vol. *la*. Many translations of this text exist in English, including Stephen Batchelor's *Guide to the Bodhisattva's Way of Life* (Dharamsala: Library of Tibetan Works and Archives, 1979), the Padmakara Translation Group's *The Way of the Bodhisattva* (Boston: Shambhala Publications, 1997), Alan and Vesna Wallace's *A Guide to the Bodhisattva's Way of Life* (Ithaca NY: Snow Lion Publications, 1997), and Kate Crosby and Andrew Skilton's *The Bodhicaryavatara* (New York: Oxford University Press, 1995).

Tsongkhapa. *The Great Treatise on the Stages of the Path to Enlightenment* (Ithaca NY: Snow Lion, 2000–2004).

——————— . *Praise to Dependent Origination* (*rten 'brel bstod pa*). For an English translation of this text, see http://www.tibetanclassics.org/Jinpa_Translation.html.

——————— . *Songs of Spiritual Experience* (*lam rim nyams mgur*). An English translation of this text can be found at http://www.tibetanclassics.org/Jinpa_Translation.html.

Index

of persons and phenomena, 67,
88
realizing, 19, 57, 58, 142. *See also*
insight
See also emptiness; self-existence
sense faculties, 50–51
Serkong Rinpoché, 79
Shakyamuni. *See* Buddha, the
Shakyaprabha (ca. 8th cent.), 157,
168n47
Shantarakshita (705–62), 155
Shantideva (ca. 8th cent.), 146, 155,
166n34
shravakas, 88
single taste, 87
six ornaments, 168n47
six perfections, 90
six sense spheres. *See* twelve links,
(5) sources
Sixty Verses of Reasoning (Nagarjuna),
83, 88, 165n26, 166n30
skandhas. See aggregates
skepticism, 13–14
sources (*ayatana*). *See* twelve links,
(5) sources
subsequent realizations, 91
subtle body, 37
subtle obscurations, 91, 166n32
suffering
birth, sickness, aging, and death,
136–37
cessation of. *See* cessation

cycle of. *See* cyclic existence
first noble truth, 18, 110. *See also*
four noble truths
"mass of," 55
meditation on, 135–37, 140
recoiling from, 19–20, 33, 96
three kinds, 20–21, 55, 127, 137
twelve links and, 30, 54, 56, 62
Svatantrika Madhyamaka, 36, 99.
See also Middle Way
systematic approach, 121–24, 129.
See also *lamrim*

tantra(s), 37, 49, 89, 130, 134,
166n32. *See also* Vajrayana
Tashikhyil (Labrang) Monastery,
47, 164n10
teacher (*guru*)
qualifications of, 130–31,
167n40
reliance on, 125, 129
See also Dharma, motive for
teacher and student
ten nonvirtues, 16
three actions, 31, 32, 53, 133–34
three higher trainings, 131, 157
Three Jewels, 7, 25–28, 95, 112, 120,
124
three natures (of Mind Only
school), 82

About Wisdom Publications

WISDOM PUBLICATIONS, a nonprofit publisher, is dedicated to making available authentic works relating to Buddhism for the benefit of all. We publish books by ancient and modern masters in all traditions of Buddhism, translations of important texts, and original scholarship. Additionally, we offer books that explore East-West themes unfolding as traditional Buddhism encounters our modern culture in all its aspects. Our titles are published with the appreciation of Buddhism as a living philosophy, and with the special commitment to preserve and transmit important works from Buddhism's many traditions.

To learn more about Wisdom, or to browse books online, visit our website at www.wisdompubs.org.

You may request a copy of our catalog online or by writing to this address:

Wisdom Publications
199 Elm Street
Somerville, Massachusetts 02144 USA
Telephone: 617-776-7416
Fax: 617-776-7841
Email: info@wisdompubs.org
www.wisdompubs.org

More Wisdom from
His Holiness the Dalai Lama

Mind in Comfort and Ease
The Vision of Enlightenment in the Great Perfection
Foreword by Sogyal Rinpoche
352 pages | ISBN 0861714938 | $24.95

Essence of the Heart Sutra
The Dalai Lama's Heart of Wisdom Teachings
Edited by Geshe Thupten Jinpa
192 pages | ISBN 0861712846 | $14.95

The Compassionate Life
128 pages | ISBN 0861713788 | $11.95

The Good Heart
A Buddhist Perspective on the Teachings of Jesus
Edited by Robert Kiely | Introduction by Laurence Freeman
Translated by Geshe Thupten Jinpa
224 pages | ISBN 0861711386 | $15.95

Imagine All the People
A Conversation with the Dalai Lama on
Money, Politics, and Life As It Could Be
192 pages | ISBN 0861711505 | $14.95